Guido Goldman

GUIDO GOLDMAN
Transatlantic Bridge Builder

MARTIN KLINGST

Translated by Brían Hanrahan

berghahn
NEW YORK · OXFORD
www.berghahnbooks.com

For Guido Goldman (1937–2020), who became my friend.
He did not live long enough to see the publication of this
biography, his dearest wish.

First published in 2021 by
Berghahn Books
www.berghahnbooks.com

German-language edition © 2001 Martin Klingst
Originally published in German as *Amerikas Mr. Germany: Guido Goldman.*

Library of Congress Cataloging-in-Publication Data
A C.I.P. cataloging record is available from the Library of Congress
Library of Congress Cataloging in Publication Control Number: 2021028081

British Library Cataloguing in Publication Data
A catalogue record for this book is available from the British Library

ISBN 978-1-80073-248-3 hardback
ISBN 978-1-80073-263-6 paperback
ISBN 978-1-80073-249-0 ebook

Contents

Illustrations

Foreword

Guido Goldman's life reflected the ruptures of the twentieth century. His life story is that of a German Jew whose family was driven from their homeland, but who then devoted his life to promoting better transatlantic relations. The story of a person who, throughout his life, was convinced that genuine mutual sympathy can only be based on mutual understanding.

Goldman was one of the central architects of postwar transatlantic relations, but until now he has remained one of the great unknown figures in the history of German-American relations.

His was a life profoundly immersed in history, but that narrative is incomplete until we hear his story, *his* own history.

Many who appear to be giants shrink away to nothing when examined more closely. But the opposite is true of Guido Goldman. The more closely you engage with him, both as a human being and a historical figure, the clearer it becomes how profoundly he shaped postwar relations between Germany and the United States.

Today—when the Atlantic seems deeper than even a few years ago—it is more important than ever that we develop a close understanding of the liberal postwar order. At a moment when that order has come under worse pressure than at any time since the end of the war.

Today, exchange and cooperation, above all, must be reinforced. As we seek to do so, who better to learn from than Guido Goldman, a man who showed understanding for people all over the world, and whose preference was always to have others tell their stories, rather than speaking of his own?

Michelle Müntefering
Secretary of State, German Foreign Ministry
December 2020

Preface

Guido Goldman did not live to see the publication of this biography. But he read every line of the manuscript and, until the last, hoped to hold the book in his hands. It almost happened: the proofs were ready for the printers when he finally succumbed to illness, just weeks after his eighty-third birthday, at his home in Concord, Massachusetts. However, Goldman's life and work continue to have a profound impact after his death, and substantial parts of the story are told here as if he were still among us.

I had absolutely no idea who Guido Goldman was when I first met him in the fall of 2006. I had come to Harvard for three months, courtesy of a Gerd Bucerius Fellowship. The Center for European Studies had kindly provided me with a workspace, a telephone, and an internet connection.

A large inscription on a wall at the Center told me that its grand premises at 27 Kirkland Street in Cambridge had been restored with a bequest from the family of Minda de Gunzburg, hence the name "Minda de Gunzburg Center for European Studies." But there was no sign, not even a tiny one, to tell me that this renowned academic institution had been founded by one Guido Goldman, who brought it into existence in 1969, then served as its director for no less than twenty-five years.

There was no Wikipedia entry (at the time of this writing, there still is none) to inform us that we owe our most important postwar transatlantic institutions, above all German-American ones, to this same Guido Goldman, who either brought them directly into being or at least helped them to grow and flourish, thanks to his energetic engagement and huge network of influential and wealthy friends who were all committed to contribute to social causes and the well-being of societies. Alongside the Center for European Studies (CES), these institutions include the German Marshall Fund of the United States (GMF), a think tank he helped establish in the early 1970s, the American Institute for Contemporary German Studies at Johns Hopkins University (AICGS), the John McCloy Scholarship program at Harvard's Kennedy School of Government, and the American Council on Germany in New York (ACG).

Back then, I also had no idea that Guido Goldman was the son of Nahum Goldmann, former president of the World Jewish Congress, who died in 1982. After World War II, it was Nahum Goldmann who negotiated with Konrad Adenauer, the first chancellor of the Federal Republic, to ensure that German reparation payments to Israel and Holocaust survivors were made. I had no idea just how many famous twentieth-century personalities had passed through the Goldmanns' New York home, from the pianist Arthur Rubinstein to the philosopher Isaiah Berlin, from Chaim Weizmann, Israel's first president, to the UN Secretary General Dag Hammarskjöld, not to mention Eleanor Roosevelt, a United Nations cofounder and the wife of President Franklin D. Roosevelt. How could I have known? Guido Goldman's last name was missing the second "n." Later he would tell me that the second "n" went astray during his US citizenship process. At the end of the citizenship ceremony, the document read "Goldman," not "Goldmann" as his parents had it. And so the name remained.

After several weeks at Harvard, all I knew about Guido Goldman, almost intuitively, was that he must be a highly regarded man, with wide-ranging influence and a substantial fortune of his own.

I felt a bit like the young journeyman from the town of Tuttlingen in "Kannitverstan," a calendar story by the nineteenth-century German writer Johann Peter Hebel. The youth goes to Amsterdam for the first time in his life, sees the marvelous buildings, ships, and goods for sale, and asks who they all belonged to. Every time, he is told "Can'tunnerstan" ("I can't understand"). "My goodness," thinks the journeyman, "this Can'tunnerstan must be a very rich and powerful man."

At Harvard, whenever I asked at the Center, the answer was the same. Who donated the modern art in the stairwell? Who gave the precious nineteenth-century European poster prints? Who was behind this or that bequest? Above all, who was responsible for the existence of the CES, and its beautiful premises here in this building, the most beautiful in all of Harvard? Every time I received the same answer: Guido Goldman.

There was one small difference, however: "Can'tunnerstan" was an imaginary figure, conjured up by the journeyman because of his lack of Dutch. But Guido Goldman was very much a real person.

Goldman's long-standing colleague Abby Collins, my Harvard point of contact, told me that Goldman had invited me to eat at a Japanese restaurant in Cambridge, as he did with most Bucerius Fellowship recipients. We had that single meeting, but then lost touch. Later, as a correspondent in Washington, DC, I saw Goldman only fleetingly. Not until late 2014, when I moved to Berlin from the United States, did I have a chance to get to know him better. Whenever Goldman came to Berlin, two or three times a year, he wanted to know about my experience of the 2015–16 refugee crisis, which I covered as a journalist for *Die Zeit* in the Balkans and North Africa. He wanted to understand how Germany was coping with hundreds of thousands of Syrian and Iraqi asylum seekers, and whether Angela Merkel could politically survive her famous statement, "Wir schaffen das" ("We'll manage this"). In addition, he sought out all the news I had from political life in Bonn. Another attendee at these meetings was Karl Kaiser, a German Harvard professor who enjoyed a close friendship with Goldman for over half a century.

I soon became aware of Goldman's burning interest in politics. Even more than political themes, however, he was fascinated by the *people* in politics, their relationships, mistakes, preferences, and intrigues. Goldman always wanted to know who could bring down whom, who might replace whom. Of course, conversation often returned to the subject of the United States, Goldman's country, which I first visited as a sixteen-year-old on a year-long high-school exchange program. At that point in time, Goldman was already teaching at Harvard, had already founded the Center for European Studies—initially called West European Studies—and was about to bring the German Marshall Fund into existence.

We had coffee half a dozen times maybe, no more than that. So in the summer of 2019, I was surprised—perplexed, even—when Goldman asked me out of the blue if I would write a book about him. He said the German Marshall Fund was to celebrate its fiftieth anniversary in 2022, and the German Foreign Ministry wanted to commission his biography in recognition of his considerable involvement in the emergence of the transatlantic think tank.

I asked for time to consider the offer. My great admiration for Goldman notwithstanding, I was undecided, doubting whether the founding of the German Marshall Fund could be an adequate basis for a biography. It would be better to write a book about Goldman himself, rather than the Marshall Fund. I asked myself who would even know about Goldman, other than the usual suspects within the tight-knit transatlantic community? Above all, perhaps: what could younger generations actually learn from Goldman and his undoubted contributions to relations between the United States, Europe, and Germany? Then a final question: apart from his life's work, what made Goldman himself an interesting person?

I had no answers that summer. I accepted the offer nonetheless, then almost immediately gave up when I realized just how many contemporary witnesses there were, not to mention the rich and extensive collection of available historical documents. But I continued with the project, drawn deeper into Goldman's life story at every step, captivated by what I read, heard, and experienced. I finally came to a conclusion: this was a story of a life that needed to be told.

Almost no one knows about Goldman. Although not without vanity, he never sought the spotlight, preferring to hang back quietly, pulling strings from behind the scenes. Nonetheless, he was a key figure in contemporary history; his life story reflects the twists and turns of a century of German, Jewish, European, and American history. His biography allows us to observe the continued impact of the Nazi era, the Cold War, and American racism; as if through a magnifying glass, we can examine the abysses, hopes, longings, successes, and defeats of the twentieth century. These twentieth-century events and emotions have not disappeared; they continue to resonate in our own world. As in a Tolstoy novel, the history of the Goldmann family is a story in which political, social, sociological pathologies—as well as some very personal ones—clash and intertwine.

The Goldmann family was forced to flee the Nazis in 1940, when they left Europe for the United States. The Goldmann family was wealthy, and their son Guido, as he himself acknowledges, led a life of privilege in New York. However, his parents took little interest in their two sons. Nahum Goldmann's passions were exclusively directed toward politics, and his own political trajectory; Alice Goldmann was largely preoccupied with herself. Despite this parental self-absorption and the absence of love, Goldman said he largely survived unscathed, ascribing this above all to the care shown to him by Ruth, his Barbadian nanny.

But there is another side to the story. Goldman's life work could never have come about without his father, including the famous name and the wide circle of illustrious friends. But if the father built the foundations, it was son who constructed buildings on top of them. Nahum Goldmann was a Zionist, passionately driven by the idea of a Jewish state in Palestine. By contrast, Guido Goldman had no specific political aim and no political program. What he did have was a keen sense for what matters.

Goldman firmly believed in the formative power of civil society institutions, in making well-chosen, effective connections between people who understand politics as a way of improving the world. Goldman was no revolutionary and he has never sought to overturn systems. He did not found movements like Greenpeace or Amnesty International. The institutions with which he was involved—the German Marshall Fund, for example—worked together with states and with groups of states in order to bring about change in governments' actions.

Like his father before him, Goldman became an intermediary among powerful people, as well as a brilliant, peerless fundraiser. Especially during the 1970s, 1980s, and 1990s, Goldman moved easily among the rich, beautiful, and influential—the network he built up was his precious capital, the foundation of his life's work.

However, it would be wrong to reduce Goldman's contribution to this. In addition to prime ministers and presidents, professors, bankers, and art collectors, Goldman mixed with activists, dancers, and social workers. He had an open, generous heart—an exceptional philanthropist and patron, he helped a vast number of people out of difficult situations, while never putting his generosity on public display. He found it a lot easier to give than to receive.

Goldman was not without ego and was quite conscious of status. He was a patriarch, happy to tell you what's what, a person who liked to keep control. But he inherited a fine, dialectical Jewish sense of humor from his father, and was quite willing to make fun of himself.

When Goldman told a story, he liked to bring in one of these Jewish jokes. A joke which was a bit problematic unless someone like him was telling it. One of his favorite jokes—often wheeled out during complex negotiations with potential donors—went like this: The Israeli finance minister is stuck in difficult talks about a construction project and needs some help. He asks his assistant to bring him three particularly clever Jews. The assistant comes back with a German, a Hungarian, and a Romanian Jew. The minister asks the German: "What is seven times five?" "Thirty-five," says the German. "Good answer," says the minister, but he wants to ask the others too. The Hungarian asks for some time to think, then says: "A number between thirty and forty." "OK," says the minister, and asks the Romanian: "So, what is seven times five?" "Well, are we buying or selling?" comes the answer.

Guido Goldman had a complex personality. Susan Rauch, a trusted friend, says that, even after decades of friendship, he could be an enigma. "A mystery," she calls him. Goldman was a restless character, easily bored. When one project came to an end, he moved immediately to the next. Josef Joffe, editor of the prestigious German newspaper *Die Zeit*—also close to Goldman for more than half a century—says he can understand this restiveness. It was simply far more interesting to set up a project or institution than to manage it when it is up and running. Another friend, the renowned sociologist Andrei Markovits, calls Goldman a "crosser of borders, a wanderer between worlds." Goldman, he adds, is "always half of something . . . an academic, but only half an academic; a businessman, a Jew, an American, a German . . . but only half."

For this reason, Goldman—who never married—had more than one family. He had many families, autonomous and adjacent—transatlantic institutions, the famous Alvin Ailey American Dance Theater (a predominantly African

American company), the *ikat* family, collectors and lovers of Asian fabrics, above all from Uzbekistan.

Think tanks, dance companies, tapestries . . . the sheer range of Goldman's activities may appear random, eclectic, even quite disjointed. In fact, this was not the case. What may have looked like loose threads had their own coherent inner logic. Henry Kissinger, Goldman's friend and teacher, says that Goldman's World War II childhood gave him an acute sense for injustice, and a profound need for reconciliation. Goldman is a "shaper" of things, says Kissinger; his life's work, in its overall scope and in its detail, has contributed to overcoming the horrors of the Holocaust, building bridges during the Cold War, and making societies a little bit fairer.

I wrote this book at the request of Guido Goldman, and with his collaboration. He read and approved every line of the manuscript before its publication. In other words, this is an authorized biography. For an author accustomed to writing freely as a journalist, this was always going to be a hazardous venture. Presented with a commissioned work, the reader might get the impression that the portrait it contains is a touched-up one. So I would like to set the record straight here. From the very start, I have striven to tell Goldman's story according to the sources available, to the best of my knowledge, and in good conscience. I do not have textual sources for everything—much is based on stories told by witnesses, whose memories may have grown deceptive with the years. Where there were doubts, I have chosen not to use these memories as sources.

Guido Goldman made his entire archive available for my research, including highly personal letters written to his parents, his brother Michael, and to many friends. I have read more than a thousand documents and carried out over one hundred interviews, including two dozen with Goldman himself. I was surprised how eager all of Goldman's collaborators were to speak about him. In the interest of frankness, however, it should be said that most of the interviewees were and are devoted to Goldman, and even the occasional critical remark always came against a backdrop of sympathy.

My agreement with Guido Goldman was that he would intervene only on highly personal issues, above all sensitive family matters. He did so only on very rare occasions.

Acknowledgments

A book like this is never produced alone; there have been many helpers along the way. Goldman's openness, my conversations and discussions with him, and the support that he offered were all essential to its completion. Critical readers have also helped, drawing my attention to mistakes, gaps, misunderstandings, and inconsistencies.

My most significant thanks go to Guido Goldman himself, who set about answering my questions with dedication and infinite patience. He never lost his calm when I failed to understand something—which happened quite frequently—or when I pressed him with follow-up questions or asked for evidence relating to something he had just said.

I also owe a great debt of gratitude to my family—my wife Ute Main and my two daughters Gianna and Lea—for putting up with so much during my six-month immersion in research and writing.

My thanks also go to Karl Kaiser, who has reviewed the book and made available his enormous stock of historical knowledge and political memories; likewise to the German Foreign Ministry for its support; to my copyeditors, Patrick Oelze and Miriam Eisleb, and my publisher, Herder, for carefully guiding the manuscript to publication. Without them, this book would not exist.

Further gratitude is owed to my wonderful American publisher, Marion Berghahn, to the magnificent translator Brían Hanrahan, to Jackson Janes who has reviewed the English edition, and to the many people from the world of Guido Goldman, and beyond, who have provided me with invaluable advice and help. My apologies if I have omitted anyone from the list: Sarita Allen, Bruce Baganz, Thorsten Benner, James Bindenagel, Hope Boykin, Meg Campbell, Cornelius Carter, Abby Collins, Maia Comeau, Jim Cooney, Richard Cooper, Kevin Cottrell, Karen Donfried, Massumeh Farhad, Helena Finn, Kate Fitz Gibbon, Dori Fliegel, Marianne Ginsburg, Sergey Gordeev, Leonie Gordon, Peter Hall, Malinda Hatch, Tom Hughes, the late Rick Hunt, Judi Jamison, Jack Janes, Joe Joffe, Jeannine Kantara, Henry Kissinger, Thomas Kleine-Brockhoff, Sergey Lagodinsky, Jörg Lau, Yannick Lebrun, Rich Ledson, Gideon Lester, Charles Maier, Andrei Markovits, Gail Martin, Michael McBride, Lois and George de Ménil, Elizabeth Midgley, John Mudd, Joe Nye, Morris Offit, Elaine Papoulias, Jeff Rathke, Susan Rauch, Harvey

Rishikof, Sam Roberts, Dacquiri Smittick, Constanze Stelzenmüller, Avrom Udovitch, Marie Warburg, Sylvia Waters, Jack Womack, Marian Wright Edelman, Christopher Zunner.

CHAPTER 1

1972 and 2019 – New Starts and Apocalyptic Moods

A MASSIVE EARTHQUAKE

Twice in recent decades, German chancellors have gone to Harvard University and made German-American history. But the history they made could hardly have been more different. Willy Brandt's visit to the university on June 5, 1972 was seen as symbolizing a new start, an optimistic stance toward the future, and faith in the United States as guarantor of the liberal postwar order. Nearly fifty years later, on May 30, 2019, Angela Merkel's visit symbolized something entirely different: the bafflement, anger, and mistrust felt by many Germans toward the country that was once the backstop of the entire Western value system.

May 30, 2019 was an important day in the US university graduation season, when the various classes of 2019 were sent into the world to the sound of ceremonial speeches. Harvard had invited Chancellor Merkel to speak to its graduating class; at almost exactly the same moment, President Trump was giving the commencement speech to officers graduating from the Air Force Academy in Colorado. The two were speaking in the same country, albeit three thousand kilometers apart. But in reality, light years separated the two speeches.

"More than ever," said Merkel at Harvard, "our ways of thinking and our actions have to be multilateral rather than unilateral, global rather than national, outward-looking rather than isolationist. In short: we have to work together rather than alone." But a very different tone came from Colorado, suggesting that the United States would no longer subordinate its interests to the sensitivities of other states. "In all things and ways," boomed the president, "we are putting America first, and it's about time." In one location, a German leader defending human rights, multilateralism, and free trade; in a word, the West. In the other, a nationalist American president taking a wrecking ball to the Western value system he despised.

On that day in May 2019, the words spoken at Harvard and in Colorado made clear what was at stake in the twenty-first century. But no one, or almost no one, had the slightest inkling of the virus that would arrive less than a year later, further accelerating the decline of the collective institutions which once formed the bedrock of the postwar order.

Guido Goldman was in the audience at Harvard to hear Merkel's speech. Just a forty-five-minute drive from his home, Harvard was his alma mater, the place where he studied, where he taught for a quarter of a century. More than anything else, this university represents the living foundation of his life's work. This was where, fifty years ago, Goldman founded West European Studies, which would in time become the Center for European Studies. The CES was the first of Goldman's wide-ranging network of German American institutes and institutions.

The election of Donald Trump in November 2016 set off a seemingly never-ending earthquake, sending shock waves back and forth across the Atlantic, disturbing the transatlantic world which Goldman had both known and helped to shape. Everything was turned upside down. The United States of America was no longer a protective, sustaining force; suddenly it represented a danger to shared ideals of freedom. People were looking to *Germany* to save the West, the country which the postwar order was established to contain. Goldman's transatlantic institutions also served to fulfill this function, as well as protecting and fostering the postwar settlement.

The postwar world order—a rugged meshwork of deals, alliances, and institutions—was meant to serve as a military, economic, and ideological counterweight to the Soviet Union, but also as a means of controlling the western German state, binding it tightly to the West's value sphere. For a long time, there was good reason to mistrust the Germans, after the horrors of World War II.

These days, seventy-five years after the war, the United States, not Germany, is the problem child of the Western world. This was Guido Goldman's view too. With every passing day, he saw the country to which his parents fled in 1940 with more and more critical eyes. Moreover, he shared these misgivings with a majority of the German population.

Goldman was also troubled by another development, fearing that some Germans' skepticism toward America might cloud their judgment and mislead their thinking, even prompting them to view China more positively than the USA. In April 2020, an opinion poll carried out for the Körber Foundation suggested that only 37 percent of Germans wanted their country to pursue close relations with the United States. Thirty-six percent felt relations with China were more important than with the USA. It bears repeating—relations with the *People's Republic of China*, a totalitarian state.

This potential self-destruction was another reason Goldman saw the West to be in danger, fearing the implosion of common value systems. He was also apprehensive for his life's work, the transatlantic institutions he created. For fifty or sixty years, these organizations have formed a strong, stable part of the liberal postwar edifice, above all the CES in Harvard, the German Marshall Fund—a unique European American think tank—and the American Institute for Contemporary Studies at Johns Hopkins. Goldman's achievements also include academic exchange programs like the CES's Kennedy Fellowships and the McCloy Scholarship program at Harvard's Kennedy School of Government.

But responsibility for the erosion of the postwar order in the West cannot be entirely laid at Donald Trump's door. For many years, the balance of international power has been shifting, with interests diverging. Guido Goldman's world—he said as much himself—was a postwar, twentieth-century world. The United States was the world's unchallenged great power, and attention was inevitably focused on Europe, which lay in physical and emotional ruins. This was the American epoch.

Of course, the United States, at the height of its powers, did not always take a burning interest in everything to do with Europe. Attention to the old continent came in waves, prompted by the contingency of events and the moods of policymakers. This was partly why Goldman created his institutions, intended to counteract the constant danger of a falling off in transatlantic relations, especially German-American ones. However, back then, it was easy enough to explain why Germany or France or the European Economic Community—later the European Union—were important for America. The same was true for Eastern Europe after the fall of the Berlin Wall in 1989.

These days, none of this is self-evident or self-explanatory. Europe, complained Goldman, has been pushed to margins, these days even Harvard seems at times to have eyes only for Asia.

Even this partly results from tectonic shifts in world politics. The United States, a waning superpower, is losing influence and importance. Under Trump, this decline is happening faster than ever, while China constantly gains in influence and importance. The United States is no longer the be-all and end-all of international relations. It is still a very powerful country, but not as powerful as it once was.

It remains unclear what all this means for future transatlantic relations, and for Europe's role in them. One thing is clear: the epoch now dawning, a post-American era, means the institutions of the postwar world will have to change. This includes the institutions established by Goldman. Most have long since begun to do so, looking for ways to reestablish the West on a new foundation.

We should not rush to conjure specters of a new Cold War. However, China presents much more than just economic competition for the West. The People's Republic of China is a systematic and strategic rival, an adversary of the liberal order. This poses difficult questions but could also inject new energy into the aging European-American partnership, although nationalists like Trump are making Western solidarity very difficult indeed.

The hopes of Guido Goldman and his colleagues—that the liberal order and its underlying institutions would bring about a lasting, irreversible convergence of states—have unfortunately proved to be a misconception.

On May 30, 2019, without citing the US president by name, Chancellor Merkel appealed to Harvard students from the steps of the Memorial Church: "Tear down walls of ignorance and narrow-mindedness!" adding that we should not "describe lies as truth or truth as lies."

More than twenty thousand people were gathered that afternoon on the manicured lawn in front of the university church. Students, professors, and family members squeezed into narrow rows of folding chairs. Some guests wore brightly colored robes, others waved American flags. During Merkel's speech, they enthusiastically leapt to their feet, with the German chancellor drawing applause and a chorus of "bravos." For Merkel, this liberal Harvard community was a hometown crowd.

Guido Goldman should have been there on the day, somewhere in the front rows, next to his old friend Karl Kaiser, a professor and a trailblazing thinker of Germany's new Eastern European policy in the late 1970s. But the hard folding chairs were too unforgiving for the eighty-one-year-old Goldman. He did not want hip pain to force him to leave in the middle of Merkel's speech: it would have seemed appalling manners.

So Goldman preferred to watch the chancellor on the large screen in the basement of the Memorial Church. Some of the church's comfortable armchairs had been astutely commandeered by members of the press corps.

Every one of Merkel's sentences was immediately translated. We should not "always act on our first impulses," she told the crowd in front of the church, "but instead take a moment to stop, be still, think, pause." The thunderous applause could be heard directly in the basement.

THE CHANCELLOR'S PRAISE

That morning, some hours before the commencement speech, Harvard had awarded the chancellor an honorary doctorate, granted by the Law School, where Barack Obama once studied. Barely had that ceremony ended, Merkel was rushed, now without her red robes, to a formal luncheon in the beautiful Widener Library. Guido Goldman was among the invited guests.

The tables in the classically decorated room were set for a festive occasion. The chancellor proposed a short toast, recalling the year 1947 and the blessings of the Marshall Plan, the flood of US dollars which had been essential to putting West Germany back on its feet. Without it, the Federal Republic would probably never have become such a free, democratic country.

Merkel recalled the figure of Willy Brandt, one of her predecessors as chancellor. In June 1972, Brandt had specifically come to Harvard to express gratitude for that same Marshall Plan. Officially named the "European Recovery Program," its billions of dollars in reconstruction aid had been announced by US foreign minister George Marshall at the university a quarter of a century before.

Brandt had brought with him a promise of 147 million deutsche marks, a gift which would establish the German Marshall Fund, a new European American think tank, and guarantee financing for fifteen years. The donation had been arranged by a familiar figure: Guido Goldman.

Goldman's great service was praised at length by Merkel in her luncheon address. Pointing out Goldman, she said: "The father of the German Marshall Fund is sitting here among us." While the guests stood and applauded, Goldman walked over to the chancellor, leaning on a cane. Deeply moved, he spoke in German, in his typically modest style: "Madam Chancellor, I never expected that you would speak such kind words of me, a rather insignificant person." It was a subject very close to her heart, replied Merkel.

Goldman, twice awarded The Order of Merit of the Federal Republic of Germany, at that point saw himself as merely an onlooker of contemporary German-American relations. He was, of course, still profoundly interested and very well-informed, but no longer held a place at the heart of things. Some years earlier, he had resigned from all important positions, handing over the reins to a new generation.

A SILVER TIFFANY CASE FOR WILLY BRANDT

Flashing back once again, moving through fifty years of history, to the moment when Brandt came to Harvard in 1972, we find Guido Goldman already an indispensable figure in the transatlantic world. Whenever he went to Germany, as he did regularly from the 1960s on, he held threads of power in his hands. Goldman was an ideas man, a crafty negotiator, a fundraiser, a manager, a master of ceremonies. Back then, there was no one else with such good connections, reaching right into the highest levels of US and German government. No one else enjoyed anything like Goldman's extensive network of the powerful and wealthy friends.

Over the decades, Goldman raised more than $100 million in donations. Among the projects supported were the Center for European Studies and the renovation of Memorial Hall, as well as various academic exchange programs. In recognition of his service, the university awarded Goldman its most prestigious award, the Centennial Medal, albeit quite belatedly.

Abby Collins, a long-standing colleague who worked with Goldman in the early 1960s, speaks of his legendary Rolodex, where hundreds of telephone numbers, addresses, and birthdays were stored. He would send little gifts to important and influential people but also to those close to him, often enclosing a framed photograph of Goldman meeting the recipient. Whether at official occasions or private parties, Goldman nearly always carried a small camera, first a Leica, later a Nikon. For some friends he was "America's Mr. Germany"; for others, he was "Germany's Mr. America."

Goldman—ever the perfectionist, occasionally a pedant—planned Brandt's Harvard visit down to the last detail, determined to leave nothing to chance. Preparations for the event involved Goldman visiting Bonn, the then capital of West Germany, on several occasions.

Goldman of course arranged a small gift in appreciation of the chancellor whose financial largesse would enable the establishment of the German Marshall Fund. Brandt's gift was a specially prepared sound recording of Marshall's legendary 1947 speech. The tape did not come in just any old box either. With typical style and panache, Goldman had arranged for a silver case from Tiffany, an appropriate container for the historic recording.

The chancellor's welcoming reception at Boston Airport, however, almost saw an embarrassing mishap. On landing, the official German aircraft made an unexpected turn and failed to stop at the agreed spot. Quick as a flash, Goldman hurried after the Boeing 707, followed by the entire welcoming committee. All were present and correct at the bottom of the steps when Brandt stepped out. In the end, it made little difference, since Brandt skipped the hand-shaking, disappearing into a black limousine, surrounded by security men.

Unlike Merkel in 2019, forty-seven years earlier Brandt had spoken indoors, in the Sanders Theatre, a wooden amphitheater inside Memorial Hall. The visit was an event in its own right, not merely a graduation speech.

Looking back, said Goldman, things were considerably more straightforward and easygoing than they are today. In 1972, both Germans and Americans were filled with great confidence, inspired with hope and vigor. That said, relations were not all smooth sailing. The United States was fighting a brutal war in Vietnam and society was deeply divided. Huge student demonstrations, sometimes violent, rocked German and US campuses, even Harvard.

Brandt expressed considerable sympathy for some of the protests, a position which did not endear him to US president Richard Nixon. Neither Nixon nor Henry Kissinger—National Security Advisor and later Secretary of State— was fond of the first Social Democratic leader of postwar West Germany, not least because of his policy toward Eastern Europe.

At the same time, the US administration did nothing to stop Brandt's new outreach to Moscow, Warsaw, and East Berlin. Outwardly, the Americans remained skeptical, says Karl Kaiser, who returned to Germany in 1968, where he taught and served as a foreign policy adviser to Brandt. But far behind the scenes, Kissinger and Egon Bahr, Brandt's point man on the new Eastern policy, set up a so-called back channel, which they kept strictly secret and which allowed the White House and the German Chancellery to discuss important matters in a timely fashion.

URGENT CALL TO THE WHITE HOUSE

Goldman enjoyed a friendship with Kissinger since their days at Harvard and regularly visited him at the White House. But unlike Kissinger, Goldman supported the new West German policy of rapprochement toward the East.

They largely kept political topics away from their friendship; each of the two took his own path on these questions.

Goldman was in Germany when the Social Democrats and the liberal Free Democrats won an overall majority on September 28, 1969, with Brandt becoming chancellor in a social-liberal coalition. He spent the election evening together with Karl Kaiser, a Social Democrat, watching election coverage on German public television. Gradually, prominent politicians began to arrive at Kaiser's home, an apartment in a lavish villa in Bonn-Bad Godesberg.

* * *

Champagne flowed that night, as it became clear that although the conservative candidate, outgoing Chancellor Kurt Georg Kiesinger, had won the most votes, the Social Democrats and Liberals had just enough seats between them to win a parliamentary majority.

But the significance of the election result was not yet fully understood at the White House. When Goldman discovered that Nixon had already congratulated Kiesinger on his election victory, he straight away called Kissinger on a secure line. "Henry," said Goldman, "you can certainly congratulate Kiesinger on coming first, but he won't be Chancellor—it will be Brandt." Nixon immediately sent a second congratulatory telegram, this time to Brandt.

German-American relations were certainly not without their tensions, even decades ago. But one thing was clear and quite uncontroversial: America was the undisputed leader of the free world. And despite differences of opinion, the states of the West had great faith in the superpower.

When Brandt officially handed over Germany's donation for the German Marshall Fund in the Sanders Theatre in June 1972, he said, in near-rapturous admiration: "America does not look away from its critical problems, but instead subjects them to unsparing debate. We regard this as proof of the country's unbroken strength. Its severity with itself is not a factor that weakens America. Rather, it reinforces our sympathies and makes our partnership stronger." For Guido Goldman, that was a tremendous statement.

CHAPTER 2

A New York Childhood

INTO EXILE

Guido Goldman was born in Zurich on November 4, 1937, the second son of Alice and Nahum Goldmann. He had one brother, Michael, twenty-six months his senior. The Goldmanns had been living in Geneva, in Francophone Switzerland, since 1933. His mother Alice was born in Berlin in 1901, the daughter of an entrepreneur, Harry Gottschalk, and his wife Emilie. For Guido's birth, Alice insisted on a German-speaking clinic, with treatment up to contemporary German medical standards. Hirslanden Hospital in Zurich was the hospital she chose; it was brand new, built in 1932, and considered to be one of Switzerland's most modern.

Nahum Goldmann was born in 1895, the son of Jewish parents from Vishnevo, in what is today Belarus. Shortly after his birth, Goldmann's parents moved to Germany, specifically to Frankfurt am Main, but for the first few years of his life, young Nahum continued to live with his grandparents, ultimately following his parents to Frankfurt in 1900.

Hitler came to power in January 1933; two months later, in late March, Goldmann and his fiancée Alice Gottschalk traveled to Palestine via Italy. A telegram had informed Nahum Goldmann that his father was dying; after Nahum's mother's death in 1930, his father had emigrated to Tel Aviv. While in Palestine, Nahum learned of the German boycott of Jewish businesses and that the Gestapo had ransacked his small office in Berlin, located in the same building as his apartment, where he had worked on the *Encyclopaedia Judaica*, a comprehensive reference work of Jewish history and culture. Friends urged him not to return. In *The Autobiography of Nahum Goldmann: Sixty Years of Jewish Life*, he wrote: "If they [the Gestapo] had found me I would probably have wound up in a concentration camp, but as it turned out I was immediately informed of this unwelcome visit and never returned to Germany during the Nazi era."

Instead of returning to Germany, the Goldmanns moved to Switzerland, settling in Geneva, where Nahum served as the representative of the American

Nahum Goldmann's bar mitzvah in Frankfurt with his parents and uncle in 1908.

Jewish Congress and the Comité des Délégations Juives. At the time, the city was an important center of international diplomacy and politics, not least since it was home to the League of Nations, the predecessor organization to the United Nations. In 1934, Nahum Goldmann also became the official representative of the Jewish Agency for Palestine to the Mandate Commission of the League of Nations. Henceforth he would be closely involved in anything of importance to do with Palestine.

One year later, in 1935, the German Reich revoked his citizenship, formally expelling him for subversive activity. However, Nahum had long suspected they would do so, and had taken precautions in good time. As a Zionist activist, campaigning for an independent Jewish state in Palestine, he already had an extensive network of contacts, stretching into the highest levels of government. Through the mediation of Louis Barthou, the French Foreign Minister, the Central American country of Honduras appointed him as consul in 1934, thus granting him Honduran citizenship. His consular passport allowed Goldmann to travel unhindered for several years while pursuing political activities.

Goldmann would also become an American citizen in 1946, and an Israeli citizen in 1964.

Harry Gottschalk, Nahum Goldmann's father-in-law, probably helped out with the Honduras deal, Guido Goldman later observed. In the early twentieth century, Gottschalk had amassed a fortune as the founder of a mail order business for state employees. At times, the company, headquartered in Berlin-Mitte, had employed up to six hundred people.

In Geneva, the Goldmann family lived in a beautiful villa close to the lake, with a nanny, a cook, and a large car with a chauffeur; they also had a second home in the center of Paris. There were no financial worries.

But in 1940, nine months after the outbreak of war, the Swiss police suddenly appeared at the family home, advising the Goldmann family to leave the country as soon as possible. Late in life, Goldman remembered how the police told the family they had information about a planned Nazi attack on Nahum. They were no longer safe in Switzerland.

It is unclear if there ever really was a plot, or if this was simply a pretext on the part of the Swiss authorities. The Swiss, said Goldman, were not unhappy to be rid of his troublesome father, preferring where possible not to antagonize Hitler.

Nahum Goldmann was a constant thorn in the side of the Nazis. In Geneva, as well as the representative of the Jewish Agency for Palestine, he was an important figure in the World Jewish Congress (WJC), which he cofounded in in 1936. Once war broke out, he had access to Hitler's greatest enemies, British prime minister Winston Churchill and US president Franklin Delano Roosevelt. In accordance with the Talmudic saying *Kol Israel arewim se lase*— all Jews are responsible for one another—the World Jewish Congress became an advocate for the rights and concerns of Jews all over the world, helping to forge an alliance against Nazi Germany.

Presented with the warning that summer, the Goldmanns made an immediate decision, not least since they believed Switzerland could be occupied by the Germans at any time. Once the policemen left, the Goldmanns began packing their bags. They left for Portugal the same day, bound for New York. Nahum Goldmann had good contacts on the other side of the Atlantic.

The family spent several weeks in Lisbon before boarding the *George Washington*. The legendary steamship had been commissioned by Norddeutsche Lloyd, the German shipping line, in late 1908, but was confiscated by the Americans in 1914, and was eventually appropriated when the United States

The Goldmann family in Estoril, Portugal en route to the US in 1940 *(Guido on right)*.

joined the war in 1917. The ship was in Lisbon to repatriate US tourists stranded in Europe since the outbreak of war, but Nahum Goldmann's contacts paid off, and he managed to acquire four tickets to New York.

Sometime later, Nahum also brought his parents-in-law, his brother-in-law, and his brother-in-law's wife across the Atlantic. But the Gottschalks were not allowed to enter the United States: the only visa they could obtain was for Haiti, where they were obliged to stay until the end of the war. At the time the United States, enforcing the Immigration Act of 1924, strictly limited the immigration of Jewish refugees.

"WE HAD A PRIVILEGED LIFE"

In New York, the Goldmanns were based in the heart of the city, in an upscale part of the Upper West Side, very close to Central Park. Their first home was in the legendary Eldorado building, a luxurious complex with two striking art deco towers, designed by the renowned architect Emery Roth in the late 1920s.

Later, they moved four blocks to an even larger and more luxurious apartment, surrounded by valuable paintings by famous artists. The walls of their home were hung with impressionist masterpieces by Monet and Renoir; later, the collection included some abstract works, notably Picassos.

In New York as in Geneva, the Goldmanns led a comfortable life, with servants and a private school for the two boys. Harry Gottschalk, their grandfather, had astutely invested part of his million-dollar fortune abroad in the late 1920s, partly in Switzerland.

"We led a very privileged life," Goldman said later, "so we were very different from most Jewish emigrants [from Europe] in New York at the time." The arrival of Henry Kissinger's family in 1938, after fleeing from Fürth in Bavaria, offers a striking contrast. In New York, the Kissingers moved into a cramped apartment in Washington Heights, a neighborhood which was home to many refugees from Europe.

Henry Kissinger, later US National Security Advisor and Secretary of State—whom Goldman first met at Harvard in 1959—worked in a factory during the day, doing schoolwork at night. Kissinger's father, a high school teacher, was unable to find a job in a city very foreign to him; his mother, Paula, the daughter of a wealthy Jewish cattle dealer from Franconia, earned money in domestic service. Her employers included the Goldmanns: she was called whenever the Goldmanns invited many Jewish guests for dinner. Her job was to make sure the food was cooked in a correctly kosher manner, and that the organization of the meal went smoothly.

Nahum Goldmann was constantly, restlessly on the move. While the war was still on, he often flew to London to negotiate with the British government about Jewish immigration to Mandatory Palestine. After the war, he went all over the world to drum up support for an independent Jewish state. He also mediated the reparations agreement between Israel and West Germany.

Later, Alice and Nahum Goldmann would mostly spend summers in Europe, where they visited the Salzburg Festival and rested at spas in Switzerland, Italy, and at Bad Reichenhall in Bavaria. In 1963 they moved back to Europe permanently, first to Geneva, then Paris. They also kept an apartment in Jerusalem.

However, during their American years, whenever Nahum was at home in New York, dinner at the Goldmann household often saw very illustrious guests, including Jewish emigrants from Europe, new American friends, bankers and captains of industry, premiers and presidents, writers, musicians and artists. Nahum, as president of the World Jewish Congress, was an important politician in his own right, well-connected among prominent people.

Guests at the Goldmanns included Eleanor Roosevelt, human rights activist, cofounder of the United Nations, and the widow of President Franklin D. Roosevelt. The apartment was visited by Chaim Weizmann, first president of Israel, and Konrad Adenauer, first chancellor of West Germany. Other guests included the UN Secretary General Dag Hammarskjöld, the philosopher Isaiah Berlin, and Herbert Lehman, the banker and Democratic politician, co-owner of Lehman Brothers, the bank whose collapse in 2008 triggered the global financial crisis. Arthur Rubinstein played on the Goldmanns' piano; the Budapest String Quartet played in their living room.

Many years later, Marlene Dietrich also became one of the Goldmanns' circle, albeit in a quite unusual way. Although they became close and lived in the same building, they never actually met in person. Nonetheless, the friendship with Dietrich was an important one for Nahum Goldmann; both his parents regularly spoke about it to Guido, so I will briefly recount the story.

When Alice and Nahum Goldmann returned to Europe and were living in Paris, they eventually moved into an apartment at 12 avenue Montaigne, the building where Dietrich also lived. She had, it also turned out, once attended the same high school in Berlin as Alice Gottschalk.

In Guido Goldman's telling of the story, one day Dietrich saw a West German broadcasting van parked outside her window, in front of the building, and presumed it was there on her account. But in fact, the concierge told her, it had come for an interview with someone named Nahum Goldmann.

That afternoon, Dietrich called Goldmann and told him that it meant a lot to her that they were living in the same building, since they had both been uprooted from Germany. "I would be delighted, Mr. Goldmann," said Dietrich, "if we could speak to each other on the phone every now and then."

Nahum was more than delighted; he had been a fan of Dietrich for years, of her great talent and beauty of course, but also of her courage and political commitment. Dietrich had opposed the Nazis from a young age, and later was a supporter of the establishment of Israel. So of course, he said, he would love to speak on the phone, but perhaps it might be better if she came over for a cup of tea? "No, my dear Mr. Goldmann," Dietrich replied, "You are welcome to telephone me any afternoon, but you will never see me." Since the end of the

1970s, she had withdrawn entirely to her apartment, hardly leaving her bed. The telephone was her one remaining connection to the outside world.

As promised, Nahum called her almost every afternoon and also sent flowers. Alice Goldmann would sometimes send her former schoolmate a delivery of good food. In return, Dietrich would send a book, or a photograph of herself. But Nahum was still saddened that he had not gotten to meet his idol. On May 31, 1982 he wrote to her: "Dear Marlene, I am dictating this letter because I would not presume to have you read my illegible handwriting (it was always bad, even before I got old) . . . In particular, I thank you for the picture. I have often looked upon it; it reminds me of the many occasions on which I watched and admired you in your public appearances. I very much regret that you refuse to receive me, I do understand your motives, although I do not agree with them."

Three months after writing the letter, on August 29, 1982, Nahum Goldmann died at a clinic in Bad Reichenhall. Dietrich sent his widow a handwritten letter of condolence: "Dear Mrs. Goldmann—I cry for you and for us, mediocre souls, Marlene." Guido Goldman said his mother was upset by Dietrich's use of "mediocre."

"WHY WAS I BORN INTO THIS OF ALL FAMILIES?"

Goldman grew up surrounded by the powerful and famous. Without the name Goldmann, without his father's contacts, he quite correctly observed, his own life's work would not have been possible. For the son of Nahum Goldmann, all of that—the contacts, the upper-class upbringing, the prosperity, his father's politics—formed one side of the childhood home. But there was another side to his childhood, which came out in the conspicuously guarded tone Goldman would use when speaking about that time. He would say it was "not bad," that his parents had never hit him or his brother, that he was always well looked after. But there was a great distance and coldness within the family; his parents were not particularly interested in each other, nor in their sons.

Of course, Alice Goldmann's letters would address Guido as "Herzelein" (My Little Darling) and "Guidomouse." His father would sign them "Your Daddy." But these were "empty phrases," said Goldman, "lacking any warmth." Even as a child he asked himself, "Why was I born into this, of all families?" He swore early on to "never be like my father and my mother."

His father, who traveled constantly, rarely saw his children. When he did, he almost never had time for them. Politics came first, always; he couldn't even remember the dates of his sons' birthdays. Guido Goldman called his father an "egotist and narcissist," only ever concerned about himself. Nahum Goldmann's autobiography serves as the best evidence for this. Over three hundred and fifty-six pages, he admiringly describes himself and his life among the powerful. His wife Alice and his sons Guido and Michael appear in one subordinate clause.

Alice Goldmann was also self-absorbed, concerned above all with her own constantly fluctuating moods. She paid little attention to her children, quickly becoming overwhelmed by home life, despite the considerable number of domestic servants. The slightest difficulty, Guido Goldman remembered, would set off a flurry of complaints: "I can't anymore, I'm so tired." The sentence was a memorable one, also distinctly recalled by Goldman's oldest childhood friend, Avrom Udovitch. Udovitch had first been friends with Michael and was constantly in and out of the Goldmann residence. When asked about Guido's mother, Udovitch immediately quoted those words, her constant lament.

At times Alice Goldmann could be exuberant: on Guido's birthday, she would give him so many gifts that the table would bend under the weight. Even Michael would get little gifts on Guido's birthday, so he would not feel left out. But she could also be dismissive and cold, telling her boys they were too childish and needed to behave like grown-ups.

Even as a child, Guido Goldman tried as much as possible to avoid his mother's mood swings, making his own way in the world. He says he was stubborn from a young age, making himself inwardly independent from his parents from early on. One evening, when he was around ten years old, Goldman was playing with his teddy bear. His parents were expecting guests and Alice Goldmann thought it unfitting that a boy his age should be cradling a cuddly toy in his arms, fearing her guests might turn up their noses. When the doorbell rang, she took Guido's teddy bear and threw it out the window.

But Goldman knew how to defend himself. While the visitors were concentrating on their aperitifs, he sneaked out of the house, fetched his teddy bear and laid it out on a cloth, surrounded by building blocks, brushes, and whatever else he could find. When the guests came and asked about his game, Goldman said: "These are the mourners at my teddy bear's funeral. My mother threw him out the window and killed him."

Even as a child, Goldman was amazingly independent and self-reliant, strengths that would benefit him later in life. But it was not easy. Alice Goldmann spent a great deal of time in bed, lacking energy. She clearly suffered from depression and great homesickness for Europe, not to mention her husband's pathological infidelity. As well as traveling around constantly, Nahum had many mistresses. The tension between their parents weighed heavily on Michael and Guido. At some point, clearly, the Goldmanns' marriage had become a loveless arrangement, a matter of convenience. But it did not begin like that.

The two had met in 1930, by way of a mutual friend, Ellen Hilb, a Jewish woman living in Berlin. Hilb was the senior secretary at the film production company UFA, in Babelsberg, where she was the assistant to Max Reinhardt, the legendary theatre and film director. She was a warm-hearted, empathetic woman, who later became an important friend to Guido Goldman, giving him important life advice. Until her death in 1992, he always affectionately called her "Auntie Ellen."

Unlike Hilb, the young Alice Goldmann, then still Alice Gottschalk, was naïve, with little interest in politics. She had Nazi friends and in the early 1920s, married her art teacher, who had joined Hitler's National Socialist German Workers' Party (NSDAP) at an early age. Alice apparently gave this fact little thought; when her friends made jokes about Jews, they would insist to her: "Oh but Lieschen, we don't mean you!"

Eventually Alice's marriage to her teacher ended in divorce, and she gradually realized the trouble that was brewing in Germany. This led her to discover her Jewish roots and Judaism in general, although strictly speaking she did not belong to the faith since Orthodox Judaism regards only those with a Jewish mother as truly born Jewish. By that criterion, only Alice's father Harry Gottschalk would count; while he had a Jewish mother, his wife Emilie did not. A complicated situation.

Goldman felt this Jewish law was particularly tragic for his grandfather Harry. He came from a family that had tried to erase everything Jewish from their lives, assimilating to the point of denying their own identity. Harry was baptized as a child and was a loyal supporter of the German Emperor. Later, he joined the Association of National German Jews. This organization, founded by Max Naumann in 1921, felt that emphasis on Jewish identity and Zionism was the cause of the hostility shown to Jewish people. Harry Gottschalk also became a member of the German National People's Party, an overwhelmingly anti-Semitic organization. He would march with other members at public marches, always toward the back, the party's token Jew: the literal German term was "Parade Jew."

Harry deliberately married a Gentile woman, Emilie. The couple had their children baptized, and they celebrated Christmas instead of Hanukkah, a full-scale Christmas, with a tree, carols, and all the rest. It must have been quite a shock for Harry Gottschalk when his daughter Alice suddenly took an interest in Zionism and began to talk excitedly about a life in Palestine. But as Guido Goldman mockingly said, his mother's new enthusiasm was less about political conviction than "campfire romanticism, a sentimentalized view of life in the desert, with camels in the sand."

In any case, one day Ellen Hilb brought Alice to see a lecture on Zionism given by someone called Nahum Goldmann, whom she described to her friend as a fascinating and handsome guy. But Goldmann proved different than Alice Gottschalk had imagined. For one thing, he was quite short, just five feet six. She was impressed nonetheless: he was a fiery speaker, who knew half a dozen languages, with a doctorate in law and philosophy.

After the event, Ellen Hilb introduced the two. Nahum Goldmann, even then a notorious womanizer, as his son Guido recounted, immediately started flirting with the pretty young woman. Alice Gottschalk was charmed and asked if she could do volunteer work for him.

Nahum was not one to miss an opportunity. It so happened he was going to Ascona for a Zionist conference the following weekend, he told her. Perhaps she would like to accompany him as his secretary? Fate took its course.

Nahum and Alice Goldmann were married in Tel Aviv in 1934. They traveled to the Promised Land for one main reason, as Nahum explained in his autobiography: "Palestine under the British mandate was the only place where a rabbinical marriage was valid in civil law." Although Nahum Goldmann had no religious beliefs, he very much wanted official religious ratification, something far more important to him than a big celebration. "I did not tell any of my friends of the marriage, which was performed in the presence of no one but the two relatives who served as our witnesses. The marriage was recorded in the Hebrew rabbinical register of Tel Aviv."

Guido Goldman thought that his parents were very much in love at this early stage, but in truth they were not well suited and never grew close. Both of them were very lonely in their own way, and they remained that way. "Loneliness and distance," said Goldman, "were the predominant feelings in our family, despite all the appearance of busy activity." Of course, this left its mark, both on him and his brother Michael. Guido Goldman had a very large number of good and close friends, but even those closest to him say they never got through to his inner core.

Toward the end of the war, in an undated letter to her husband, Alice Goldmann described her inner emptiness. Nahum was abroad, yet again. From the letter, it seems he had previously told his wife that the situation in Europe and the fate of the Jews had depressed him very much, often leaving him feeling very alone. "I can only be a companion for you," Alice Goldmann replied coolly, "but everyone has to find things out for themselves, and go their own way, all the way to the end. The sooner you realize that in the end you will always be alone, the better it is."

Goldman's parents could not find a way of being together, but neither could either leave the other. In 1963, they moved back to Europe together. Nahum Goldmann was constantly traveling during those years too, often in Germany and Israel, and had girlfriends almost everywhere. But as far as Guido could remember, there was never talk of divorce. His mother was "too afraid of being alone." His father, he would add sarcastically, would never give up his wife's money, "his house bank."

The relationship between Guido and his brother was also difficult. Michael, said Guido, probably suffered more than he did from his parents' coldness and his mother's emotional roller coaster. Michael became mentally ill, apparently no rare thing on the Gottschalk side of the family.

In early childhood photos, Michael and Guido are often in each other's arms, joking and dressing up as Native Americans. During the long holidays, they would travel together to Penacook summer camp in New Hampshire and camp out in Wadleigh State Park on the shores of Lake Kezar. That was the best time of the year, said Goldman: "our weird parents were in Europe. We could relax and be free."

Guido, although two years younger, was always in charge. He helped Michael with his homework, later helped him with college work, and explained to him how things worked. "He was like the older brother," said Avrom Udovitch, their shared childhood friend, "Guido always took responsibility and made all the important decisions." It stayed that way until Guido Goldman's death.

One anecdote illustrates Goldman's early determination and his fierce will. When the brothers first went off to summer camp at Penacook, their parents gave them a stack of pre-addressed and stamped envelopes: the sons were meant to send regular reports to Europe to reassure their parents that everything was OK. But their tent was damp at night, and the glue on the envelopes sealed them closed. Guido just used the glued envelopes as postcards, each time writing briefly: "Hello, we're fine, best regards Michael and Guido."

The parents were none too pleased with these sparse reports. The following summer, Nahum insisted that his sons send a telegram every week. But Guido Goldman simply would not do it. "No other child had to do that," he asked, "so why should we?"

The refusal to send the telegrams was, of course, Guido's idea. Michael only went along with it because his brother promised him that he would do all the necessary fighting with his father. It was not long before a telegram from Europe arrived. It contained just four words: "Please confirm well-being, Father."

Michael and Guido as young boys.

For Guido, this was just more "typical father": Nahum Goldmann lavishly spent his money on himself, but with his sons kept costs down by avoiding unnecessary words. So Guido sent four words back: "Well-being hereby confirmed, Guido."

The older the two boys got, the more alienated they became. Guido played basketball, did well at school, and had many friends, with whom he regularly went to stay. Michael was more of a loner, with difficulties at school. In contrast to Guido, he was a highly political youth, dreaming of a life on a kibbutz. He became involved with Hashomer Hatzair, a left-wing Zionist youth organization.

This was where Michael met Udovitch, who was working as a volunteer at Hashomer Hatzair's New York headquarters. For Udovitch, who grew up in modest circumstances in Canada and had to get by on ten dollars a week in New

Michael in high school.

Guido in high school.

York, the Goldmanns' life seemed like paradise. They had a large television in the living room and a refrigerator full of food: there was always plenty to eat, and only the best. When Udovitch first met Michael's brother Guido, around fifteen at the time, he thought: "You couldn't get more American: he was tall, strong, with huge feet and purple-checked trousers, and all he talked about was basketball."

Child of an upper-class European family but more American than any American? For Dori Fliegel, a friend from Cambridge, who knew Goldman better than most, this was not a contradiction. Although Goldman's spirit was European through and through, Fliegel nonetheless says his friend was "quintessentially American." By this, Fliegel says, he meant that Goldman was "unfinished," in the best sense of the word, always open to new things, with "high tolerance for ambivalence" and a "love of the unpredictable." Not a person to lead his life according to anyone else's script.

This is an excellent description, as it explains both Goldman's tireless search for new challenges and his extraordinary audacity. Had he lacked this final trait, he would probably never have achieved so much in life, in so many different fields.

Goldman was quite apolitical in his younger years, traditional and conservative in his habits. More the young dandy than a hippy or a revolutionary. Udovitch says Goldman liked to make fun of his brother's political activism at the time, mockingly calling Michael and Udovitch "radical leftists" and jokingly threatening to report them to the FBI. Udovitch did not have much of a relationship with Guido Goldman at that point, he thought the younger brother too conventional, too smooth. They became friends years later, while Udovitch was studying history at Columbia and Yale and Goldman was studying politics at Harvard.

Meanwhile, Michael was gradually losing his way in life. He studied for short periods in the United States and at Sciences Po in Paris. He tried his hand at acting. In the 1960s, he married an African American dancer from the Alvin Ailey American Dance Company, moved to Paris, had two children with her, then got divorced. He was also permanently broke. Even a wine business, which he expensively established in Paris, did not make a penny. Guido Goldman said Michael never worked a full day in his life.

At some point, Guido's older brother went completely off the rails, drinking heavily and taking drugs. In California, he left the scene of a car accident. Although the incident was not his fault, he escaped jail only because Guido hired him the most expensive local lawyer he could find.

Because their parents continued to give in to Michael, failing to take a clear line with him, Guido increasingly distanced himself from the family. This made his mother very unhappy. But she was torn, as ever. At times she would express understanding for Guido's annoyance, even share it. At other times, she bitterly accused him of selfishness.

This was the chaotic emotional world in which Guido Goldman grew up. Even decades later, he could hardly escape. In July 1977, his mother wrote a revealing letter to her son, at a time when she was almost seventy-six, her husband eighty-two, and he almost forty. "Dear Guido," she wrote, "I am so sad because I feel that you have feelings of hatred. I know N's [Nahum's] mistakes—but he has a lot of lovable sides to him, while you only see the dark sides to his personality. I cannot understand what you have against me. I can only guess. You were such an indescribably lovely person . . . Since you are the closest person in this world to me, I suffer a lot from this, and yet I am completely helpless and cannot do anything for you."

"FORTUNATELY, THERE WAS RUTH FROM BARBADOS!"

Considering this home life, it would have been no surprise if Goldman had run aground like Michael or become cold and self-centered like his parents. But in fact he was the exact opposite: empathetic and caring, with a big heart. So what made him different? Goldman said he owed it to nannies, especially to Ruth. "Fortunately for me," he said, "there was Ruth from Barbados."

Michael and Guido's first nanny, while the family was still in Switzerland, had been a young woman called Ditty. It was Ditty who washed the boys, pushed their baby carriages beside Lake Geneva, fed them, and sang them lullabies. When the family emigrated in 1940, Ditty had to stay behind. Guido, at two and a half, was very sad about this: for a long time, he resented his parents for not taking Ditty with them.

In New York, the family soon hired Ruth, a Black woman from the Caribbean island of Barbados: she was smart, warm, and very loving. Guido clung to her, preferring to sit with her in the large kitchen, along with the cook and the maids. "There was always such a warm, happy atmosphere there," he said, "very different to my parents' living room, a few yards away."

Through Ruth, Goldman learned about racial discrimination as a child; his eyes were opened to the injustices of the world. Goldman attributed his involvement in the civil rights movement to Ruth, and particularly his later work with the Alvin Ailey American Dance Theater.

At the time, racism, ethnic, and religious discrimination were not limited to Nazi Germany. When the Goldmanns came to the United States in 1940, certain human beings were vilified because of how they looked, where they came from, or what they believed in. They were also worse off under the law. This affected African Americans, but also Native Americans and many Asians.

Jews too could find it difficult to find a job or to obtain a place at university; in some places, they were prevented from buying property or even from settling in certain parts of the United States. But no group was discriminated against as systematically and brutally as African Americans.

At the time, lynchings took place almost every week, Black people were forced to go to separate schools and universities, could not drink from the same public water fountains, and were forced to give up their seats to white people on buses. WHITES ONLY signs were common in restaurants and shops, and not only in the states of the Deep South. At the time when the Goldmanns moved to New York, most American states strictly forbade "mixed marriages" between whites and African Americans.

Racial segregation also prevailed in the Goldmanns' apartment house on the Upper West Side. There were two elevators, with the grander one reserved for whites only. Back then, all residents and all visitors were white, as were some of the staff, including Mrs. Beringer, the Goldmanns' governess for a time. Even the elevator operator, who wore a uniform and pressed the buttons for the residents, was an Irishman named Harry.

There was also a second, less fancy elevator, to be used by nonwhite people, in other words people like Ruth. Since Ruth had to take the Goldmann sons everywhere, then pick them up again, Guido came to know the second elevator well. When he was with Ruth, he also had to take the elevator for nonwhites.

One Sunday when he was ten years old, Goldman was returning with his parents from an opera matinee. He was not fond of these cultural excursions: he felt the atmosphere was too stiff, the singing too artificial. This day, as always, the parents took the first elevator, but Guido ran straight to the second elevator and rode up to the family apartment.

Nahum Goldmann was extremely annoyed and demanded that his son explain this nonsense. "With Ruth, I always have to take the second lift," said young Guido, "she's never allowed in yours. You always talk about how badly

Jews are treated, but this is just the same. If you are committed to the equal treatment of Jews, you must do the same for Black people." His father was taken aback, but immediately began to campaign to end racial segregation in the building's elevators, with ultimate success.

Goldman also sided with Ruth against his mother. For a few days in the early summer of 1947, it was so hot and humid in New York that the asphalt melted in the streets. Alice Goldmann wanted to surprise her sons and bought an air conditioner for the children's room, a rectangular box to be installed in the window frame.

"Will Ruth get one too?" asked Guido immediately. "No," said his mother, "do you have any idea how much these things cost?" Air conditioning systems were still a rarity, and extremely expensive. Guido said he thought this was deeply unfair. He and Michael would soon be in summer camp, he said, and his parents in the relative cool of Europe, but Ruth would have to spend hot months in her small, stuffy one-room Brooklyn apartment. "I don't know anyone who buys an air conditioner for the maid," said his mother, exasperated. "Then I don't want one either," said the boy, telling his mother that she could send the box back to the store right away. The result: the air conditioner stayed, and Ruth got one too. Again, young Guido had prevailed.

Because he went through life with open eyes, always questioning, Goldman early on developed a keen sense of what was wrong with society. Even as a child he wanted to give away what he had in abundance. Whenever the Goldmanns had guests who did not eat kosher, a huge roast was served, with all guests well fed. Alice badly wanted to avoid any impression that her portions were small, so a second roast was always put in the oven. The servants were allowed to take from this: there was always plenty left over.

Young Guido, who would sit in the kitchen with Ruth on these occasions, felt this was an enormous waste and wanted Harry the elevator operator to get something too. He liked him and always brought him a large plate of meat from the roast.

Ultimately, it was his mother who provided Goldman with his crucial relationship with Ruth. Despite her many shortcomings, Alice Goldmann almost always chose nannies well. There was only one exception: Mrs. Beringer from New York. But here too, Guido took matters into his own hands.

Alice Goldmann always spoke German with her sons. But this was too difficult for their father. Nahum Goldmann was impatient by nature and wanted Guido and Michael to answer his questions immediately. Since they both now spoke far better English than German, he preferred to speak to them in English.

Alice Goldmann did not agree with this, fearing that Michael and Guido could forget their German. She searched for a German-speaking governess. The "nurse," as was the term then, was supposed to speak German with the boys, while teaching them virtues like punctuality, diligence, and obedience. Alice Goldmann was nothing if not German.

On this occasion, Mrs. Beringer was selected for the role. She lived in New York and, as Guido Goldman remembered it, was a Nazi. Mrs. Beringer would take the Goldmann boys to the infamous Café Geiger on 86th Street. In the late

Former Chancellor Konrad Adenauer and Alice Goldmann in the family's Jerusalem apartment (May 1966).

1930s, the café had been a popular meeting place for the "Bund," an association of German-American Nazi supporters, and even after the war, patrons would greet each other with "Heil Hitler."

Guido and Michael Goldman hated Mrs. Beringer, who yelled and ordered them around, and wanted the old "witch" gone. But their mother steadfastly ignored her sons' complaints. So Guido Goldman hatched a plan to get rid of their terrible nanny as soon as possible. He took a large bucket, filled it with hot soapy water, sloshed it over the linoleum floor in his room then started screaming at the top of his lungs. Frau Beringer came running, slipped, broke her elbow—and quit the job. "That was the end of our Nazi governess," Goldman joked later in life. Mrs. Beringer's successors were far nicer.

A BAR MITZVAH TRICK

Nahum Goldmann was a very important person in the Jewish world, but it had little to do with religion: he was a political and cultural Jew, not a religious one. In this, he was like Kissinger, who came from an Orthodox Jewish family but says of himself that he is Jewish by ethnicity, not belief.

Guido Goldman said that from an early age he felt Jewish only when he encountered anti-Semitism. For example, as a child he discovered that Jews like his family were banned from buying or renting in some apartment buildings. Or when children in the summer camp shouted "kike" at him.

"Kike" was and is a common slur used against Jews in North America. There are two main explanations of the word's origin. One theory claims that in Slavic-speaking countries, Jewish surnames often ended with "ki" or "ky." Another theory claims the abusive term originated at Ellis Island, the island in the Hudson River which was once the main arrival point for immigrants to New York. A number of Jewish immigrants, mainly from Eastern Europe, were illiterate or unable to use the Latin alphabet, but refused to fill in the immigration form with the usual letter "X," since they regarded the X as representing a Christian cross. So they filled in the boxes on the form with a circle instead. The Yiddish word for circle is *kikel*, for a small circle, *kikeleh*. Thereafter, officials on Ellis Island called Jewish immigrants *kikel*, *kikeleh*, and ultimately "kike."

However, this kind of vilification was quite unusual during Goldman's childhood and youth. In Manhattan, he attended Birch Wathen, a very progressive private school. Most of the girls in the school came from Jewish families, but among the boys, Guido and Michael were the only Jews.

Andrei Markovits, the child of a Romanian Jewish family, a professor of sociology at the University of Michigan, and a good friend of Goldman's since they studied at Harvard together, says of him: "He has always set himself up in two directions at once: he is Jewish when he is confronted with anti-Semites, but when he came up against his father, often a hypocritical figure, he was a non-Jew."

Nahum Goldmann, who spent the first six years of his life with his grandparents in the shtetl of Vishnevo, described himself in his autobiography as a mixture of eastern European Judaism and Western Enlightenment. "In Vishnevo," he wrote, "I took it for granted that I was a Jewish child." The residents of the shtetl were almost exclusively Jews. For this reason, he explained, he never felt the "Jewish fear of the overwhelming power of the non-Jewish world," and so did not feel offended when someone in Frankfurt insulted him as a "dirty Jew." The experience led Goldmann to conclude that "the sureness of a Jewish consciousness can spring only from a strong living reality, never from teaching or preaching."

Michael and Guido did not experience this "strong living reality" in the United States. Nor did their father pass it on, since he by now he was living in a quite different world. Nahum Goldmann, the boy from the shtetl, had known everything about Judaism, spoken Yiddish, studied the Torah, and known religious and cultural laws better than anyone. But growing up in Frankfurt from the age of six, he came under the influence of the non-Jewish German intellectual world. "For German Jews, but also for millions of Eastern European Jews," he once wrote, "Europe only meant German culture. Their minds contained Lessing and Schiller, Kant and Hegel, Goethe and Heine, but not Racine or Molière, Shakespeare or Milton, Pascal or Locke."

Nahum Goldmann was enthusiastic about German literature and philosophy, and the music of Beethoven, Mozart, and Bach. He often sat in front of the gramophone, deep in thought, and would probably have liked to be a musician himself. He was saddened when his sons proved unable to sing a note in tune, and when piano and clarinet lessons failed to awaken their musical sensibility.

Nahum Goldmann did not have to act out his Judaism, it formed part of who he was. Avrom Udovitch says that Guido's father's origins meant his

Jewish identity was a matter of course, never questioned. "But that did not apply to his two sons, who lacked Jewish experience of their own."

The Goldmanns did not pray at the table, did not go to synagogue, and did not observe the Sabbath between Friday and Saturday evenings. Although they served kosher food to guests, they never ate kosher themselves. For breakfast, Nahum favored a large plate of eggs and sausages.

Christmas was regularly celebrated in the home, but Passover was observed only a couple of times during Guido Goldman's childhood, because Nahum loved to sing Hebrew songs. But every Christmas, Nahum ordered that the tree be set up in the furthest corner of the apartment, not wanting it to be the first thing his guests saw on entering. He feared that his Jewish visitors—as president of the World Jewish Congress he received many in the course of his political work—might take offense at the family's Christian traditions.

Guido Goldman despised this hypocrisy, feeling his father was only concerned with himself and with keeping up appearances. His Judaism, says his son, was in many ways a sham. Nahum Goldmann married a non-Jewish woman and had many non-Jewish lovers, but he threw Michael out of the apartment when he announced that he would marry Jacqui, also non-Jewish. When Guido was considering marrying a non-Jewish woman, he took him aside: "If you do that," he said, "you will be damaging my career."

As a child, Guido Goldman hated this kind of duplicity. When he was twelve, his father wanted him to learn Hebrew and take Torah lessons from a rabbi so the family could hold a bar mitzvah when Guido turned thirteen, the great Jewish celebration which marks a boy's religious coming of age.

Guido Goldman could see no point to this: there was nothing in it for him, unless he could negotiate some quid pro quo with his parents. He had always wanted a dog, his greatest dream. At one point, at his urging, his mother bought him a dog in Gimbels department store but got rid of it immediately when it became pregnant.

The loss of the dog broke Guido's heart: he decided never to trust his parents again, and always in the future to get guarantees on their promises. This was the beginning of Guido Goldman the tough negotiator and skillful tactician. As a twelve-year-old, he developed the skills of a shrewd businessman, which would be of great use in his life's work.

When his father asked him again about the bar mitzvah, Guido said he was not yet really sure, maybe he was ready, maybe he was not. Nahum Goldmann

Guido and his father in the 1960s.

explained that the occasion was important to him, then asked if perhaps a gift might help him make up his mind. "Yes, a dog," came Guido's rapid-fire response. "No problem," said his father, "we can do that."

But young Guido was smart, and wary. He feared that once the bar mitzvah was over, the promised dog would never materialize. So he insisted: "I don't want to have the dog after the party, I want it three weeks beforehand." But this annoyed his mother. A puppy three weeks before the party was not going to happen, she said, not wanting an untrained puppy wandering among the one hundred guests. "Okay," said Guido, "then you'll have no problem, I'll have no bar mitzvah."

His father gave in immediately: he was planning to invite important Jewish friends and acquaintances to his son's celebration, it was unthinkable to cancel the bar mitzvah. Guido would get the dog half a year before the big event.

But that was not the end of things. Of course, Guido did not want just any dog. Certainly not a pocket-sized dog, he wanted the largest one possible. His parents insisted on a small one. They ultimately agreed to a cocker spaniel, but Guido cunningly chose an English cocker spaniel, knowing very well that they are larger than most dogs of that breed.

To ensure the puppy was house-trained for the bar mitzvah, it stayed in the care of the breeder for five more months. Exactly three weeks before the celebration, Guido and his father brought the dog home to the Upper West Side. At the celebration, the boy proudly showed off his English cocker spaniel to the one hundred invited guests. In fact, he was carefully showing the dog around in case his parents changed their mind after the party.

The question of the family's Jewishness—how much and what kind— was a constant subject in the home, and a constant source of conflict. Alice Goldmann, unlike her husband, grew up with no Jewish tradition. She knew well that her children suffered from the religious duties imposed on them by their father. In March 1969, after Nahum had again complained about one of Guido's "German girlfriends," she wrote to her son, telling him he should not let his father influence him. In life, she went on, good relationships matter, not whether someone is Jewish or not.

Alice Goldmann's letter to her son perhaps best explains this dilemma: "Daddy has not conveyed any Jewish spiritual or religious values to you," she wrote, adding that his attitudes were "dubious and hypocritical." She herself came from a family of "assimilators," with no religious conviction, she said. "Of course I have a lot of German in cultural terms, which I have involuntarily passed on to you. . . In an intellectual and cultural sense we are no longer Jews. I find real piety wonderful. It must come from the heart and give life a shape. Then it forms a firm family bond which can give support and radiate warmth. . . Unfortunately we have no tradition—a great loss, but it does give us freedom of choice."

But Nahum Goldmann also felt these contradictions, torn between his intellectual distance from Judaism as a religion and his desire for greater religious connection. In Jerusalem in October 1967, he was troubled by the possible spiritual void in his family. In a rare moment of self-criticism, he wrote to his son: "Religion, if it is not narrow-minded and fanatical, has its meaning and great value. It is the spiritual foundation on which the family is built. Many families produce a community, then a people, a state. Perhaps one must have abandoned and lost tradition to the degree our family has to suddenly understand what is actually missing."

EVERYONE DANCES THE HORA

The Goldmanns may not have been religious, but Nahum Goldmann's political Judaism shaped their family life. From early in the twentieth century, his actions had had a single goal: the foundation of an independent Jewish state in Palestine. As much as Guido quarreled with his father, he had great respect for his political achievements, highlighting two in particular: negotiating reparations for Israel and Holocaust survivors, and his father's leading role in the partition plan for Palestine, where he pulled some strings which made the difference.

Nahum Goldmann wanted a Jewish state, but he also believed that peace with the Arabs was only possible if the Palestinians also had a state. On Saturday, November 29, 1947, the moment came for the United Nations General Assembly to adopt the partition plan, under Resolution 181 (II). The British mandate over Palestine was repealed, with a Jewish state and an Arab state to be established in the territory. Nahum Goldmann was not alone in hoping this might end the dangerous conflict between the two peoples, a hope shared by the majority of the world community. As we all know, things have turned out quite differently.

Guido Goldman remembered the week before that crucial, historical Saturday. The UN was and is based in New York, his home city. It was not clear if the partition plan would pass, there was strong opposition, and the necessary two-thirds majority rested on a knife-edge.

In fact, the General Assembly was supposed to vote on Wednesday, the day before Thanksgiving. But Nahum Goldmann needed more time to deal with a few hesitant delegates, and urged Trygve Lie, then the UN Secretary General, to postpone voting to Saturday.

Goldmann knew Lie—a Norwegian diplomat—well and knew he supported the partition plan. The Secretary General agreed to the postponement and Nahum Goldmann spent three days working the phones non-stop. Above all, he turned to Jewish friends in Latin America, asking them to put pressure on their governments. He learned from UN sources that some Latin American delegates were still undecided. By Saturday morning, he was sure he had the

Nahum Goldmann and Chaim Weizmann at Zionist conference in 1933.

two-thirds majority. Shortly afterwards, partition was approved by thirty-three votes to thirteen.

The victory was celebrated long and loud at the Goldmann home on the Upper West Side. Over a hundred guests came, including Chaim Weizmann, who would be elected Israel's first president fourteen months later. Like Nahum Goldmann, he was born in what is now Belarus. Abba Eban was another guest: in 1970, through Goldmann's mediation, Eban would be the first Israeli foreign minister to visit the Federal Republic of Germany. Moshe Sharett was also in attendance: he would serve as Israel's second prime minister, between 1953 and 1955.

There was plenty to eat and drink. Days beforehand, Alice Goldmann had asked Paula Kissinger to prepare the party, making sure to have enough kosher snacks on hand. The atmosphere was lively, with music playing. Chaim Weizmann and others happily danced the hora, the traditional Jewish dance.

This was the day Nahum Goldmann's dream finally came true. After the foundation of the state, he often spent time in Israel, moving into a large penthouse on Achad Haam Street, an elegant thoroughfare, where Konrad Adenauer would later come to visit him. In the 1960s, he was granted Israeli nationality, in addition to his other citizenships. Nahum Goldmann even briefly considered running for prime minister as the Labor Party candidate.

Alice Goldmann was often in Jerusalem, but her sons rarely visited. Michael, who had once wanted to live on a kibbutz, settled in Paris before later moving to California. The two centers of Guido's life were Harvard and New York.

The establishment of a state did not settle the matter of Israel. The issue continued to loom large in the Goldmann family in the following decades, because of Nahum's continued political activities but also because partition failed to bring peace to the Middle East.

Above all, Guido Goldman felt alienated from the increase in Israeli nationalism and the country's settlement and occupation policy. He did not think that Israel, after victory in the Six Day War in June 1967, should permanently control the West Bank, the Gaza Strip, the Golan Heights, and East Jerusalem, nor that it should gradually annex territories.

When United Jewish Appeal, a pro-Israel charity, today known as the UJA-Federation of New York, approached Goldman with a request for donations, Guido said that he would give a donation, including retroactively for years gone by, and with interest, as soon as Israel agreed to return occupied Palestinian land. "I was sure," he said later, "that this moment would not come and the promise would not cost me a cent."

Goldman shared his growing alienation from Israeli politics with many Jewish professors at Harvard. The sentiment became still stronger after the 1973 Yom Kippur War. Israel came close to being wiped out: as a consequence, beginning in 1977, Israelis began to vote in governments that were more and more right-wing, and quite uncompromising. This was painful for Nahum Goldmann, who had closer links to the left-wing Labor Party. "In his worst nightmares," said his son, "my father would not have thought it possible that Israel would one day be ruled by a right-wing nationalist like Benjamin Netanyahu."

Israel's future continued to preoccupy the Goldmanns: how could it not, as tentative hopes for peace grew, only to be trampled on again? This produced a constant roller coaster of emotions, reflected again and again in the letters of the Goldmann family, which are an impressive barometer of the mood in the Middle East, a historical document of constant ups and downs.

Guido Goldman went to Israel for the first time in the 1950s. It was many years before he returned, but he visited again in 1962 and was impressed by the country. His parents were pleased. "I received your two, very long letters," Alice wrote to him in English on July 6, 1962, "and we both are very happy about everything you did write. I am glad that you like Israel. Somehow we all belong there, even if we do not live there permanently."

Just five years later, Alice Goldmann was very worried. On May 28, 1967, a few days before the Six Day War, she wrote to her son: "Dear Guido, you can imagine how the situation in Israel depresses me, and not just me. This time everyone seems to be afraid of a major conflict, and this fear also means an understanding that insensitive unscrupulousness is no use to anyone now. Israel will remain a constant focus of danger, even if this time there is no war. The hatred which has accumulated among the Arabs over many years could ignite at any time. This is so palpable when you live there, in a world that is immensely contained, like a ghetto, and where a terrible hostility is breeding beyond its borders. Daddy has always known this: this is what his critique is based on."

In November 1975, hope flared up again. Nahum Goldmann told US Secretary of State Henry Kissinger, a friend of his son, that he was now quite optimistic about the Middle East situation. The Israelis, he wrote, were "becoming much more moderate and are much more ready to accept a complete withdrawal—always with the exception of Jerusalem—in which case they would obtain a real peace agreement."

Two years later, the Goldmanns were again depressed: the government of the center-left Mapai party was voted out of office, with Menachem Begin taking over as prime minister. Concerned, Guido Goldman wrote to Zbigniew Brzeziński, a friend from Harvard, now National Security Advisor to President Jimmy Carter: "Dear Zbig: As many Americans, I have grown more concerned about prospects for peace in the Middle East since the election results in Israel."

However, just a few months later, confidence was flowing once more. In November 1977, Anwar as-Sadat, the president of Egypt, made a surprise visit to Jerusalem, offering Egypt's archenemy a comprehensive peace treaty,

Pierre Mendes-France, Menachim Begin, Nahum Goldmann, and Anwar as-Sadat on his visit to Jerusalem in November 1977.

including the recognition of Israel's right to exist. Sadat named his conditions for this: complete withdrawal of Israel from occupied territories, including East Jerusalem, and the creation of a Palestinian state within safe and internationally guaranteed borders.

The Goldmanns were in Jerusalem at the time, and Alice Goldmann wrote euphorically to Guido: "Here you can imagine, how people are excited about the unexpected visit of Sadat. . . . All were sitting at the TV, who were not waiting in the streets—for the arrival of Sadat. It shows how much the people here are waiting for a breakthrough. I think it was a historical moment, even if nothing will show up right away." Less than a year later, Israel and Egypt concluded the Camp David Agreement, assisted by the mediation of US president Jimmy Carter. Anwar as-Sadat and Menachem Begin were awarded the Nobel Peace Prize.

The moment of happiness was brief. Forty years later, at the time of this writing, the Palestinians still have no state of their own. Israel, supported by President Donald Trump, has announced it will permanently annex large parts of the occupied West Bank. In the summer of 2020, Israel suspended annexation plans so as to establish diplomatic relations with the United Arab Emirates. But the Palestinians remain excluded.

At the end of his life, Nahum Goldmann was disappointed, less and less inclined to return to the country he cofounded. In November 1981, already weakened by illness, he wrote sadly to a Jewish friend in New York: "Dear Carmella, what you tell me about Israel confirms the impressions that others have shared with me. They are a people in an absolutely crazy frame of mind, and I fear the consequences will be very dire."

In early April 1982, when the Goldmanns were at home at 12 avenue Montaigne, the Israeli embassy in Paris was bombed. Shortly afterwards an Israeli diplomat was murdered, with Lebanese terrorist groups taking responsibility. That May, over a hundred rockets were fired at Israel from the south of Lebanon, and early June saw the attempted assassination of the Israeli ambassador in London. Sometime later, Israeli troops marched into Lebanon, eventually advancing to the outskirts of Beirut. A regional conflagration threatened.

On August 13, 1982, Nahum Goldmann published an article critical of the invasion. "Israel—Where Are You Going?" appeared in *Die Zeit*, the respected German weekly newspaper. The article is a document of disillusionment.

Goldmann sharply attacks Menachem Begin, the conservative prime minister, warning that a militarily superior country like Israel might win battle after battle, but in the end it could "win itself to death."

Israel, he warns, "is as good as alone in world public opinion," with only the support of the United States. It ran the risk of becoming permanently alienated from the Arab world. "When you consider," he writes, "the enthusiasm and admiration with which Israel was received by Jews and non-Jews in the first ten years of its existence, we can only be deeply disappointed about the weakening of the country's privileged position."

Nahum Goldmann's contribution to *Die Zeit* was his political testament. Two weeks later, on August 29, 1982, he died in a clinic in Bad Reichenhall. His son Guido was there with him at the last. Despite his alienation from Israel, Nahum Goldmann's last wish was to be laid to rest on Mount Herzl, the Jewish national cemetery in Jerusalem.

CHAPTER 3

Guido Goldman's Extended Family

A HOUSE FOR ALL HIS FRIENDS

In late August 1982, Guido Goldman was on Vinalhaven Island when he received news that his father had been taken to a hospital in Bad Reichenhall, with his health failing dramatically. His parents had gone to the Bavarian spa town for a rest cure.

For many years, Goldman had spent summers on the small island off the coast of Maine; in 1975, he bought a property overlooking the ocean, a spacious building with nearly a dozen small bedrooms and almost as many bathrooms. He had originally purchased the house with his brother Michael in mind. In the 1970s, Michael lived in Paris with his wife Jacqui and their

Guido's summer house on Vinalhaven, Maine (acquired in 1975).

children Stephane and Maya and, although the marriage was already in crisis, he wanted a place on the New England coast where they could come together in the summer with Jacqui's large American family.

Even though the two brothers had little in common, Guido always helped his brother out. It was not easy to find a suitable house. The first one he chose was rejected as too small and uncomfortable. Goldman sought advice from Zbigniew Brzeziński, a friend from Harvard, then a professor of political science, later National Security Advisor. Brzeziński had a large mansion in Northeast Harbor, on the coast of Maine, and let Goldman know about various properties for sale or rent in the neighborhood. What made the area particularly attractive was an exclusive country club with tennis courts, offering everything his brother might want for himself and his family. Michael Goldman was a keen tennis player.

Brzeziński wanted to invite the Goldmans around but observed that there might be an unfortunate problem. He referred to it, as Goldman later recalled, as "the American plague." Michael's wife, Jacqui, was African American, and Brzeziński told Goldman that the country club would not accept Black people as members, not even in limited form for the summer months. This was in 1974, a decade after the Civil Rights Act, which guaranteed Black Americans the same rights as whites.

Brzeziński said that he was willing to fight the country club on the issue, as long as Michael wanted this and felt strong enough to endure the struggle. "No chance," replied Guido Goldman, knowing his brother to be an unreliable character. Through acquaintances, Goldman finally found an appropriate property, on Vinalhaven Island. But his brother's family did not spend a single summer in the house.

However, Goldman himself took a liking to the place on the Atlantic shore and turned it into a gathering place for his many friends and acquaintances, a perfect place to maintain his contacts. There was much networking and back-scratching on Vinalhaven Island, between the Udovitchs and the Hoffmanns, the Collinses and Lindemanns, the Fliegels and Lesters, the de Ménils and Sacklers, to name only a few. At one point, Lord Soames, Churchill's son-in-law, stopped by, staying for two weeks at the Goldman place.

Until he sold the house in the late 1990s—at a considerable profit—Goldman held court for six weeks in Vinalhaven every summer. He also made a significant amount of money through skillful operations on the real estate market.

Guido's 42 ft wooden boat, built in 1928, the "Marina S."

Every year, Goldman brought tons of groceries to the island, a highly complex logistical operation. He went on boat and bicycle tours with his guests, organized picnics on neighboring islands and, in the evening, screened American films on the wall using a small projector. When video technology arrived, he bought large numbers of VHS tapes, building up an extensive film library.

There was always a large basket of lobsters floating at the end of the jetty; every few days, the local fisherman would fill it with fresh catch. People could just help themselves, there was plenty of lobster to go round. The fisherman and his family of course came to eat at Goldman's welcoming table—they also helped around the house, kept an eye on things in the stormy autumn months and during the long winter. They made a good living for many years thanks to Goldman. Even when he sold the property, he continued to look after this fishing family. This was one of Goldman's distinguishing characteristics: he cared about his employees' and associates' well-being, even when they no longer worked for or with him.

"MY FATHER'S COFFIN ARRIVED ON A NORMAL SCHEDULED FLIGHT"

On Vinalhaven Island, Goldman was entertaining guests on the day in August 1982 when he learned his father had been hospitalized. He told them things looked very bad for his father, packed a suitcase, had the lobsterman take him to the mainland, took the next plane to Frankfurt and from there drove a rented car to Bad Reichenhall. No matter how distant his relationship with family, he showed up when he was needed, which was often.

So as not to frighten his father with an unannounced bedside visit—Nahum Goldmann was very afraid of death—Goldman whispered to him that he was on his way to a conference and would only stay a moment. The doctors told him his father would die soon, but that "soon" could drag on for weeks, maybe even a month or more.

The next day, Goldman flew to Paris to sort out a few things in his parents' apartment. As soon as he arrived, Hella Moritz, Nahum Goldmann's long-time secretary, called him in an agitated state from Bad Reichenhall, telling him that his father's condition had rapidly deteriorated. Moritz was Nahum Goldmann's right-hand woman, always close by. In Paris, she lived in a small apartment in 12 avenue Montaigne, the same building as the Goldmanns and Marlene Dietrich.

Hella Moritz was an enthusiastic opera goer and the Goldmanns had given her tickets for the Salzburg Festival, which was taking place at the time. The city of Mozart, although across the border in Austria, was only twenty minutes by car from Bad Reichenhall.

Guido Goldman immediately flew back to Bavaria, where he kept watch by his father's bedside. His father kept moving in and out of consciousness, and was confused, not knowing if he was in hospital or at his hotel. The following morning, Sunday, August 29, he suddenly asked for a new blue shirt he had bought a few weeks earlier.

"Why?" asked Hella Moritz. "Because I want to go to *Cosi fan tutte* in Salzburg this evening," replied Nahum, who had hardly eaten for two days. "Unfortunately that won't work this evening," Moritz said, but continued: "Dear Dr. Goldmann, if you have your supper today, you can go to the opera tomorrow." Nahum Goldmann was annoyed by this, obviously feeling patronized. After grumbling "You always have to be right!" he looked out the window, said "I'm moving to another hotel!" And then died. At that moment, his son thought: "What could be a nicer death than thinking that you are at a hotel and on your way to the opera!"

Goldman went to tell his mother that her husband had died. Alice Goldmann remained composed, speaking in the foyer of the hotel to Hans-Dietrich Genscher, foreign minister in Helmut Schmidt's government, also a fan of the Salzburg Festival.

Goldman then called Edgar Bronfman in New York, his father's successor as president of the World Jewish Congress. Bronfman was one of the four children of Samuel Bronfman, the legendary Canadian spirits manufacturer, who made billions as the founder of the Seagram Company. Edgar's sister was Minda de Gunzburg, a close friend of Guido Goldman for many years. After her death, her husband and two sons donated $15 million to the Center for European Studies, founded by Goldman, allowing it to move into the most beautiful building in Harvard in the late 1980s.

Bronfman wept when he learned of Nahum Goldmann's passing and offered to transport the coffin to Jerusalem in his private plane. According to Jewish custom, the deceased person should be buried within twenty-four hours if possible, because the soul can only ascend if the corpse is correctly laid to eternal rest. However, this period is interpreted less narrowly for Jews who die abroad and want to be buried in Israel.

Another Jewish tradition is that the dead must not be left alone until they are buried. This custom goes back to biblical times, when Jews died in the desert during the flight from Egypt and wild animals attacked the corpses of the dead.

Apart from Guido, no one in Bad Reichenhall could uphold this tradition, so important to his father despite his lack of religious belief. His mother was too weak, his brother Michael was in Paris. Guido kept watch in the hospital until his father's body was collected the following day.

Although it was a sad occasion, Goldman was in his element, doing what he did so well, doing what had made him so successful: planning, networking, communicating, arranging, organizing. He had a phone installed to call his father's closest associates around the world, using a list stating exactly when he could reach each person in their particular time zone. He spoke with Sigmund Warburg and Alain de Rothschild, both bankers, as well as with the German chancellor Helmut Schmidt and Marion Gräfin Dönhoff, editor of *Die Zeit*, all good friends of his father.

Every few hours a nun in a habit would poke her head curiously around the door. The hospital was Catholic, and the nuns did not know Jewish death customs. Goldman felt obliged to explain things and wrote a brief statement during the night, which he gave to the nuns the next morning before the undertakers arrived. Before his own death, Goldman was still smiling at the fact that he, an unbeliever, found himself in the strange position of explaining Jewish religious laws to Catholics. "The nuns," he would laugh, "were deeply impressed by my piety."

Edgar Bronfman returned the call, profoundly saddened. It turned out that the coffin would not fit in his Gulfstream, so he offered to charter a Boeing 737 at his own expense. But Goldman refused. It would cost at least $100,000 and he could imagine the headlines: "Goldmann Transported in Private Boeing!"

His father, says Goldman, always had a reputation for living large: expensive apartments, Cuban cigars, the finest tailor-made suits, and a luxury Bentley sedan. No need to top that now that the man was dead. "The coffin with my father's body," Goldman told Bronfman, "will arrive in Israel on a scheduled El Al flight."

Nahum Goldmann never liked to fly El Al when he was alive; he found the service poor. But now, his son told Bronfman, was the perfect time. There could hardly be a better image for his father's farewell than his coffin at Tel Aviv airport in front of an El-Al aircraft bearing the Star of David.

Guido Goldman also arranged the funeral services, and everything related to them. Who else in the family could do it? But a few outstanding difficulties remained. Goldman had learned that Orthodox rabbis in Jerusalem could, at the last minute, refuse to allow his father to be buried on Mount Herzl, where they had authority over the civilian cemetery. During his lifetime, Nahum Goldmann repeatedly crossed swords with Orthodox rabbis, often saying jokingly to Guido: "When you meet an Orthodox rabbi, keep a close grip on your wallet."

Mount Herzl was named after Theodor Herzl, first president of the World Zionist Organization and the founder of political Zionism. In fact, his successors to this office had the right to be buried on Mount Herzl if they wanted. Nahum Goldmann had been president of the World Zionist Organization from 1956 to 1968.

A few years earlier, Nahum Goldmann had told his son he wanted to be laid to rest at the cemetery on Mount Herzl. Wisely, in view of possible resistance, Guido Goldman had taken precautions in good time. As soon as his father expressed the wish, he asked Eric Gornitzky for advice. Gornitzky, a prominent Israeli lawyer, put together a fifteen-page report listing in fine detail the parts of the World Zionist Organization's statutes which gave its former presidents the right to be buried on Mount Herzl.

That moment came on September 2, 1982, when Nahum Goldmann was laid to rest on the hill above Jerusalem, just hours after US president Ronald Reagan presented a new Middle East peace plan. It was as if Nahum Goldmann was still directing events, even on the day of his funeral.

Mourners came from far and wide. Edgar Bronfman brought a dozen mourners in his Gulfstream. Israel's president Chaim Herzog stood by the grave, along with Shimon Peres, the leader of the Labor Party, later both a prime minister and a president of Israel. Peres had been born in the same Jewish shtetl, Vishnevo, as Nahum Goldmann.

Guido and his Welsh Springer Spaniel, "Sherman," on Vinalhaven in the 1980s.

Only Israel's then prime minister Menachem Begin withheld his respects to Goldmann, who had been a persistent critic. As if seeking to harm Goldmann even at the moment of his death, Begin scheduled a cabinet meeting for the day of the funeral, at which he harshly rejected Reagan's peace initiative.

In the weeks that followed, messages of sympathy from all over the world arrived at Harvard for Goldman. Nahum Goldmann, always a controversial figure, left behind a large void in the political world. "Dear Mr. Goldman," wrote former German chancellor Willy Brandt, leader of the Social Democrats, "It is important to me to convey to you personally my condolences on the death of your father. His efforts for peace and appeals to reason have not been listened to nearly well enough. But we will have to return to much of his thinking if peace—especially in the Middle East—is to have any chance."

Brandt's message to Goldman was a sincere one, written from the heart. Guido Goldman had often crossed swords with his father and had been personally hurt by his selfishness and coldness. But Goldman was well able to distinguish between his father's failures as a human being and his political significance, recognizing that Nahum Goldmann's life's work was of great political importance around the world.

In her obituary, Marion Gräfin Dönhoff pointed out that Nahum Goldmann, in London on December 6, 1951, had "been the first Jewish person (after World War II) to speak to a German as the official of one country to another."

In negotiations with Chancellor Konrad Adenauer, Goldmann had laid the foundations for the Reparations Agreement. "Reparations" is a terrible word, quite wrong in the context, as if it were possible to make up for the murder of millions of Jews, Sinti and Roma, homosexuals, people with disabilities, and those opposed to the regime. Thanks to Goldmann's mediation, the Luxembourg Agreement was finally concluded on September 10, 1952, between Adenauer, Israeli prime minister David Ben-Gurion and the Jewish Claims Conference. What was then West Germany, the Federal Republic, pledged to pay billions to the State of Israel and to Jewish victims all over the world.

There were protests against the agreement, including in Israel. Understandably, many Jews wanted nothing more to do with Germany, and had serious objections to "blood money" from Bonn, fearing that Germany would pay its way out of its irredeemable guilt, as if buying a medieval indulgence.

Nahum Goldmann, however, defended both the agreement and his own mediation. In *My Life as a German Jew*, a book published in 1980, he wrote:

"I have always been of the opinion that peoples should not decide on their relationships through their emotions; their interests demand that at some point they find a form of coexistence, without allowing themselves to be dominated by emotion, however justified that might be. Every foreign policy decided on emotion sooner or later ends in catastrophe." This was also the belief of both Henry Kissinger and Goldmann's son Guido, both exiles from Nazi Germany.

Given recent political upheavals, which have included the emergence of politicians who are both democratically elected and authoritarian—including Donald Trump, Viktor Orbán in Hungary, and Benjamin Netanyahu in Israel—Nahum Goldmann would probably no longer speak merely of "interests." To do so would run the risk of defining these solely in terms of power politics. Like his son, Nahum Goldmann would instead speak of "value-bound interests," in other words, policy based on the principles of the liberal international order.

It was also to Nahum Goldmann's credit that he refused to indiscriminately ascribe "collective guilt" to all Germans for the crimes of the Nazis. Instead, he emphasized "collective responsibility" for the atrocities and their results, insisting that no one could, nor should, ever evade this responsibility.

This important distinction was later emphasized by Guido Goldman when Daniel Goldhagen published his book *Hitler's Willing Executioners: Ordinary Germans and the Holocaust*, which rekindled dispute over the question of collective guilt.

On September 11, 1982, two weeks after Nahum Goldmann's death, his son defended his political legacy, reiterating his criticism of Israeli government policies. In a *New York Times* opinion article, Goldman backed Reagan's peace plan, which Begin so brusquely rejected on the day of his father's funeral. The article sharply criticized the Israeli prime minister for his stubborn refusal to yield ground. But the piece also took various Jewish groups in America to task, as key supporters of the Israeli prime minister.

In his article, Goldman said his father understood that Israel could not survive without American support in the form of money and military assistance. "But what . . . saddened Father in more recent years was the way in which American Jewish organizations too readily aligned themselves with the Israeli Government in resisting any pressure for a change of course in Israel's approach to the Arab world. . . . It would be a great pity if American Jews were, through blind loyalty, merely to echo the views of an angry Israeli Government."

A TRUST FUND FOR JACQUI

Michael Goldman was always somewhat overshadowed by his brother Guido, the younger by twenty-six months. Even as a young man, Guido had many friends, and was sociable, athletic, and popular. He was elected class president in high school, studied at Harvard and later taught there; he established transatlantic institutions of lasting value and received numerous prestigious awards for his service. He was an art collector, a savvy real estate investor, and became a wealthy man by acting as a trustee for rich American families, including the Bronfmans, de Gunzburgs, and de Ménils.

Michael had things harder in life. Lacking stamina, he dropped out of Columbia University after a few semesters, then transferred to the Institut d'études politiques in Paris, known as Sciences Po, only to drop out again.

In the early 1960s, Michael married Jacqueline Walcott, a gifted African American dancer with the famous Katherine Dunham Company, who later joined the no less famous Alvin Ailey American Dance Theater. But soon after the wedding, she abandoned her career as a dancer and had two children. The family moved to Paris, where they bought a spacious two-story apartment around the corner from the Latin Quarter. But Michael never really got a foothold in life; this also affected the relationship between the two brothers.

Michael Goldman is an intelligent man, and he could be funny and entertaining. At times, he surrounded himself with interesting people, bringing much pleasure to his brother Guido, who befriended some of these people himself, as with the singer Harry Belafonte and his first wife Julie Robinson Belafonte, and Frances Taylor Davis, first wife of the jazz legend Miles Davis, whom Goldman met at his brother's wedding. The Belafontes were groomsmen on the day, with Miles Davis playing the trumpet. At the time, Jacqui was very close to both Julie Belafonte and Frances Davis, both also dancers.

Michael and Jacqui Goldman were divorced in 1980. There were disputes over maintenance and common property. But Guido Goldman forced the Goldmann family to establish a trust fund of half a million dollars to provide for Jacqui and the children. "They are part of our family," Guido Goldman insisted to his parents. At his insistence, Avrom Udovitch, the brothers' mutual childhood friend, was appointed trustee. By that time, Udovitch had become one of the most respected historians in the United States, the director of the Department of Middle East Studies at Princeton. Eighty-seven years old at the time of writing, he continues to look after Jacqui Goldman and her children Stephane and Maya with great care.

From childhood on, Guido Goldman had always been the active, caring member of the family. Although he was not close to either his parents or his brother, he would let no one down. On the contrary, he constantly looked out for them.

Alice Goldmann was quite helpless after the death of her husband and sought advice and support from Guido. In November 1982 she wrote: "Dear Guidolein—thanks for everything! What would I do without you and your care?" As her strength gradually waned, Goldman moved his mother to Zumipark, an elegant retirement and nursing home on the outskirts of Zurich. From her suite, she looked out onto pastures filled with peacefully grazing sheep, with the snow-capped Alps in the background.

Guido flew in regularly from the United States. He also paid for family friends to make the trip to Zurich, so his mother—increasingly suffering from dementia—would receive other visitors besides himself. In the summer of 1992, one wrote: "From our point of view, the Zumipark represents the optimum possible care that an old person could wish for." From the director to the nurses, from the assistants to the restaurant service, everyone at Zumipark showed great courtesy to Nahum Goldmann's widow. The friend continued: "Not many people can afford this kind of retirement home, and those who can should consider themselves lucky." Alice Goldmann died on November 27, 1994 and was buried next to her husband on Mount Herzl.

Of course Guido Goldman also took care of his brother, by now seriously ill with dementia, living in a Los Angeles nursing home, with no assets of his own. The costs of his care are paid for from a trust fund set up by Guido, also administered by Avrom Udovitch.

Guido Goldman said that whenever he thought about himself and his family, the image of "Mother Courage" came to mind. The character in Brecht's eponymous drama hauls a covered wagon loaded down with her children. Goldman saw the play for the first time as a teenager, and remained preoccupied with it. "I am not 'Mother Courage'," he said, "but the heavy wagon does symbolize my parents and Michael, whom I have dragged with me over the decades."

A FISHER OF MEN AND A PHILANTHROPIST

Goldman had no children of his own, and never got married or had a relationship. There were various reasons for this. He himself says that he was put off by the example of his own parents' marriage. In addition, he was too busy for that kind of permanent connection with another human being. Finally, he feared passing on the burden of mental illness which plagued his mother's family.

Perhaps the narrowness of convention and the conservatism of the social climate meant Guido Goldman could never find the right partner or form of life for a long-term relationship. He did not talk about it much himself; he was not at all a person to speak openly of his inner life or feelings. His closest friends, who have known him for decades, say he has always been a wanderer and searcher, making difficult to get involved with one family, one person, or one partner, whether a woman or a man.

His friend and sociologist Andrei Markovits described him very accurately. "Guido," he said, "is vulnerable, a restless spirit, always a little bit on the run." Until recently, he commuted constantly between his various apartments and houses, constantly seeking to create something new. Quickly bored, he never lingered long in company: at some point, whether at his home or a restaurant, he would politely let his guests know that the evening had come to its conclusion.

Goldman liked to have people around him, Avrom Udovitch observed, if possible a constant stream of different people. The historian says that Goldman was the most entertaining, generous, and caring person he ever met. Andrei Markovits, Joe Joffe, Karl Kaiser, and long-time friends Susan Rauch and Marie Warburg are of the same opinion. Guido Goldman was a doer and a patron, a philanthropist, a people's person and a fisher of men.

From his childhood on, Goldman helped countless relatives, friends, and acquaintances, assisting numerous people in need or in a tricky situation. A few examples: one time, Goldman paid off a hard-up friend's mortgage so she would not lose her home. On another occasion, he paid for the best possible lawyer for an acquaintance involved in a labor dispute. He allowed a friend, a professor not living at Harvard and with only a small teaching salary, to stay at his home during the semester to save him expensive Cambridge rent.

He paid for the private school of an English godson, and for a class trip to Italy for the son of the couple which looked after his house, and regularly sent "Aunt Ellen" a check. He gave a close friend who lives in the mountains an interest-free loan to buy a neighboring property, so no one would block her view of the marvelous landscape. He bought Joe, his assistant of many years, an apartment, intended as life insurance so he would be taken care for when Goldman was no longer around.

He paid for expensive dental treatment for the daughter of the lobsterman on Vinalhaven Island, and every few years would bring his ex-sister-in-law Jacqui, who lived in France, to New York to watch a gala event at her former dance theater. On these occasions, Goldman would also fly in Jacqui's old dance friend Frances Davis from Los Angeles, at his own expense. In addition, he paid the rent on Davis's apartment until the end of her life; the great dancer was left with little money after divorcing her husband Miles, an abusive husband.

In recent decades, it was mostly African American friends who benefited from Goldman's largesse. Ruth, his Barbadian nanny, he said, opened his eyes to ubiquitous, structural racism. His commitment to the Alvin Ailey American Dance Theater, a mainly Black dance company, taught him, unfortunately, that little had changed for the better since his days with Ruth. With Barack Obama the United States had their first African American president and now, with Kamala Harris, their first vice president of color.

"But Black people," said Goldman, "are still discriminated against on a daily basis, in all areas of life: education and health care, on the job market, voter registration or if they end up in the clutches of the police and the courts." Dancers run a high risk of injury, and their bodies are often completely worn out after two or three decades. Black dancers are often left with nothing at the end of their performing career.

Goldman provided financial support to Katherine Dunham—the legendary dancer and civil rights activist, pioneer of Black Dance and founder of the Dunham School of Dance and Theater in 1945—until her death in 2006. He did the same for Vanoye Aikens, star dancer with the Katherine Dunham Dance Company in the 1940s and 1950s, who died in Los Angeles in 2013 at the age of nearly ninety-one.

More than any other institution, Guido Goldman supported the Alvin Ailey American Dance Theater (see Chapter 11 for more about this company). He felt particularly drawn to the dancers after being appointed to the ensemble's board of trustees in 1994. He helped the highly talented Hope Boykin through difficult financial times; every year he bought Yannick Lebrun, star dancer, a plane ticket to visit his family in his native French Guiana. Goldman covered naturalization costs for dancers from the Caribbean, Latin America, Africa, and even France, and often contributed cash to help dancers build a new professional life after their dance careers were over.

It was particularly important to Goldman to support dancers who were marginalized because of their social background, skin color, or sexual orientation. Goldman met many such dancers at the Alvin Ailey American Dance Theater. He hosted the wedding of Sam Roberts and Michael McBride, both dancers and both gay, and gave another couple money so they could build a small house in St. Louis.

Goldman was wealthy, but his resources were not inexhaustible. Had he had children of his own, he said, he would not have been able to be so generous to others. But his "children" are the people at the Center for European Studies, the German Marshall Fund, and the Alvin Ailey American Dance Theater. They all form part of the huge extended Guido Goldman family.

Looking at this family through Goldman's eyes, his parents and brother Michael look like the people he was more or less forced to take under his wing. The dance theater is undoubtedly the child closest to his heart; of the "children," the German Marshall Fund went furthest in life, while Goldman felt a particularly intellectual connection to the Harvard Center, his "firstborn," as it were.

CHAPTER 4

Early Years at Harvard

THE TRUTH WILL OUT

In the summer of 1955, Guido Goldman faced the choice of which university to study at. He had excellent grades in high school and had been elected class president, an extremely solid basis for successful US university applications.

But for Goldman, there were only three universities in the running: the small but excellent Dartmouth College in Hanover, New Hampshire; Wesleyan College in Middletown, Connecticut; and Harvard, one of the best universities in the world, located in the New England city of Cambridge, very close to Boston.

Goldman applied to all three. His father of course wanted his son to go to Harvard, and he approached his friend Felix Frankfurter to request a letter of recommendation, in the hope of further strengthening Guido's dossier. Felix Frankfurter was a judge on the US Supreme Court, among the most brilliant lawyers of his time and—particularly helpful—a graduate of Harvard Law School. Frankfurter had never met Guido, but he did him the favor.

Soon after, Goldman was invited to Cambridge for an interview. Because of the recommendation from Frankfurter, the interview was personally conducted by the head of the admissions department, Wilbur J. Bender. He immediately asked if Goldman was aware of the letter of recommendation. Goldman nodded, whereupon Bender asked how well he knew Frankfurter.

At first, Goldman did not know what to say. If he told the truth—that he has never met Frankfurter in his life—the recommendation letter would be worthless. If he said the opposite, his lie might be exposed. On the spur of the moment, Goldman chose the truth. A fortunate choice. Dean Bender immediately read him the first sentence from Frankfurter's letter: "Nahum Goldmann, whom I appreciate very much," wrote the Supreme Court judge, "has asked me to make a recommendation for his son Guido, whom I do not know." Goldman was enormously relieved.

All three universities accepted his application, but Goldman's preferred option was Wesleyan, not Harvard. The college is less than two hours by car from New York, and also offered Guido a scholarship and other perks. The seventeen-year-old felt flattered by Wesleyan's energetic interest.

Shortly before registration deadline, while they were attending a picnic, Guido Goldman explained his thinking about the college question to Robert Berks, a family friend. Berks was a respected sculptor and the creator, among other things, of the Albert Einstein Monument and the large bronze sculpture of John F. Kennedy in the foyer of the Kennedy Center, both in Washington, DC. At that time, he had just completed a bust of Nahum Goldmann. Berks was horrified to hear that Guido Goldman wanted to go to Wesleyan rather than Harvard. He frankly gave the young man a piece of his mind: "If you do that, you are no longer my friend."

"TWENTY-FOUR CARAT THINKERS"

Goldman arrived at Harvard in August 1955. Almost all the new freshmen were brought to the university by proud parents, an old American tradition. But Nahum was on his travels yet again and Guido's mother had no interest: she only ever visited her son at Harvard once, at his graduation in the early summer of 1959.

So Guido Goldman drove up alone in his red Plymouth Cabriolet. This was technically against the rules: students were not supposed to bring a car, since the university feared that students might get behind the wheel drunk after a party and cause an accident. The university also preferred that students not flaunt their wealth.

Showing off was the furthest thing from Goldman's mind: he only wanted the car to drive home to New York. So he parked it far away in the parking lot of Harvard Business School, on the other bank of the wide Charles River, well out of sight.

Goldman signed up to study politics and government and moved into Matthews South dormitory on campus. All male first-years were accommodated on campus for their first two semesters, an old American tradition.

At Harvard, even the freshmen are spoiled. Unlike other universities, they don't have to squeeze into a single room for several people. Instead, they share small apartments, with three people living together in two bedrooms, a living room, and a bathroom. When asked by the university who he would like to move in with, Goldman told them he would like to live with an African

American and a foreign student if possible, hoping that the mix would lead to more interesting conversations. Ironically, however, Goldman was put together with two students who, like him, were both Jewish and from New York. Goldman thought the university probably thought that anyone making a request like his must be extremely insecure and should be put with students from a similar background.

Goldman had little in common with his new roommates. One was tedious and eccentric, the other was a brilliant thinker who many years later would become a famous astrophysicist, but who at the time plunged into schoolwork to the exclusion of all else.

After their first year, all students had to move out of freshman housing. For the next three years, until graduation, Goldman would live in Winthrop House, a few steps from the Charles River, a building which has hosted many famous names, including John F. Kennedy. Life is comfortable at Winthrop House, a spacious building where Goldman first shared a three-bedroom suite with three other students, thereafter one with four bedrooms, a living room and a bathroom.

This was a period when Goldman formed many lifelong friendships. In 1956 he met John Mudd, a student of politics, whom he encountered via an old school friend from New York. Mudd's parents and his eldest sister Emmy became a kind of surrogate family for Goldman; he spent a lot of time with her and felt well taken care of at the Mudd home. At spring break, the Mudds took him on a trip to Haiti and the Virgin Islands. Years later Emmy would take him on a visit to the picturesque New England town of Concord, where she then resided.

Goldman fell in love with Concord, which is an easy drive from Harvard. In 1978, he bought an imposing home in the town, located in a large park on a wooded hill above the Concord River, surrounded by small lakes and ponds. Here the only sound was the twittering of birds, with every now and then a deer breaking through the bushes, while in autumn the trees turned deep shades of red and orange. A place for silence, reflection and contemplation. This is probably why, of the many houses that Goldman bought, this was the only one he did not resell, and where he lived until his death in November 2020.

John Mudd and his wife lived close to Concord, and every few weeks Goldman invited them to dinner in Cambridge. Jack Womack, another close college friend from the early Harvard years, would always attend.

Unlike Mudd and Goldman, Womack grew up in modest circumstances. His father was a postman from Norman, Oklahoma, but a very well-read man, who attached great importance to education. This helped his son to escape the lonely expanses of the Midwest: a scholarship enabled him to attend a good high school in St. Louis, Missouri, where he was discovered by Harvard. Through its "diversity program," the university tried to offer talented students from less well-off families the chance of a good education.

In their last academic year before graduation—senior year—Goldman and Womack lived in adjacent apartments in Winthrop House. By opening up the connecting doors, they created a shared apartment. Years later, both would teach at Harvard, and Womack, a historian and expert on Latin America, would eventually receive tenure.

Mudd, Womack, and Goldman went out into the world, studied in various places in Europe, moved here and there and everywhere for professional commitments. But for decades, Harvard remained the shared center for all three of their lives. Goldman became a kind of godfather to Womack's daughter Liza, while Mudd made Goldman a trustee for his children. The Mudd family was one of the early sponsors of Goldman's Center for European Studies, and continues to donate money from time to time.

Goldman's early years at Harvard saw another momentous encounter: when he moved to Winthrop House in 1956, the great Stanley Hoffmann became his tutor and academic supervisor. Another American university tradition at the time was for young professors to live under the same roof with students for a while, taking care of their intellectual and personal well-being. Hoffmann, only nine years older than Goldman, was already an expert in political science, and a highly gifted teacher. A specialist in French politics, the history of ideas, the sociology of war, and the postwar history of Europe, Hoffmann could cast a spell over students like no other teacher.

Hoffmann was born in Vienna in 1928, the son of an American and an Austrian Jewish woman. His parents divorced shortly after his birth, and he survived the Nazi era with his mother in France. In Paris, he studied and taught at Sciences Po, among other places. In 1955, Hoffmann was offered a position at Harvard and moved to the United States, where five years later he became naturalized as a US citizen.

Hoffmann had a large fan base at Harvard, including Goldman and John Mudd. Dinner at Winthrop House was often a sociable affair, and Guido

Guido Goldman with his teacher and mentor, Stanley Hoffmann, at the Center for European Studies.

Goldman became Hoffmann's constant table companion. The student from New York, quite unpolitical as a teenager, had by now learned to enjoy arguing about America and Europe, God and the world. To some of his fellow students, he may have seemed somewhat precocious, but he himself would say he was neither particularly intellectual nor a great academic talent: "It was only thanks to my father and his illustrious guests that I was able to join in discussion everywhere. I picked up the best bits and pieces of conversation and then kept passing them on."

Mudd and Goldman hung on Hoffmann's every word. "We soaked up his knowledge like a sponge," says Mudd. "But apparently Hoffmann also appreciated talking to us, especially with Guido." Hoffmann, who had remained more French than American, was passionate about European and international politics. Of course he knew who Nahum Goldmann was, and listened with interest when Guido spoke of his father and the prominent contemporary figures who frequented the Goldman family homes. At some point, Goldman drove his teacher to New York in the red cabriolet to introduce him to Nahum Goldmann.

* * *

Hoffmann and Goldman became good friends. The younger man admired his professor's intellect and his ability to acquire knowledge through reflection alone. Goldman himself was more politically and practically oriented and focused primarily on government and political science, taught by Henry Kissinger or Zbigniew Brzeziński. Both were professors at this point, but many years later would enter politics themselves, first as advisers then as senior office holders.

Hoffmann also had great appreciation for Goldman. Later, he would tell him: "Guido, you are one of the most important people in my life." Goldman's generosity, influence, and entrepreneurial talent were of enormous benefit to Hoffmann as a professor at Harvard.

The two could hardly be more different, almost opposites: the tall, enterprising, extravagant Goldman and the small, ascetic Hoffmann, entirely devoted to scholarship. However, almost a decade and a half after first meeting at Winthrop House, this mismatched pair would establish West European Studies, and later its successor organization, the Center for European Studies. At Harvard, Goldman and Hoffmann combined to write new pages in the history of the university.

In his first Harvard semesters, however, Goldman was disoriented in academic terms, not quite sure of the final goal of his studies. He was interested in almost everything, and with so many great minds for teachers it was difficult for him to decide on a major.

At the time, Harvard was home to a group of "twenty-four carat thinkers" as Josef Joffe, the journalist and editor of *Die Zeit*, called the cohort of professors then at the college. Joffe, born in Poland to Jewish parents, came to Harvard himself in the late 1960s, where he became friends with Goldman.

During and after World War II, Harvard was a magnet for Jewish scholars who had escaped the Holocaust in time, or who managed somehow to survive.

Guido Goldman, in a way, felt himself their soulmate and part of their generation, especially if that concept is taken not to mean a similar age group, but people with comparable life experiences, as suggested by the sociologist Karl Mannheim.

NO IDEA OF POLITICAL THEORY

Hoffmann and Kissinger were not the only Jewish professors with whom Goldman studied at Harvard. He brushed up on his German with Egon Schwartz, especially grammar and spelling. He would later enjoy a lifelong friendship with Schwartz, a Jewish literary scholar, originally from Vienna.

The political scientist Judith N. Shklar, also Jewish, born in 1928 as Judita Nisse in Riga, Latvia, was another teacher at Harvard, an eminent liberal theorist and the first woman to receive tenure in the department of government.

Shklar taught political theory, but Goldman avoided her classes. "Judith Shklar was a strict teacher," he says, "and I was extremely bad at political theory, completely without talent." But in retrospect, he should have overcome his inner resistance; more than a decade later, when Goldman took his doctoral examination, political theory was one of the two written and four oral exam subjects. His examiner in the subject: Judith Shklar.

Goldman was nervous about the exam; having a doctorate is a prerequisite for teaching at Harvard, and Stanley Hoffmann had already suggested they jointly offer a course in European politics. So what to do? In a crash course, Goldman acquired a basic knowledge of political theory, choosing as a topic the forerunners of Marxism, a subject on which little had been written, making it easier to improvise in the exam. In his preparation, Goldman was helped by Erich Goldhagen, a brilliant young scholar and, as Goldman says, "in very good shape, in terms of political theory."

Goldhagen was also a European Jew, from Romania, who had survived the Holocaust in the ghetto in Chernivtsi, a city now in Ukraine. His son is Daniel Goldhagen, the historian whose controversial book *Hitler's Willing Executioners* would unleash a new debate in the mid-1990s about German collective guilt, a debate in which Goldman would also play a role.

Ultimately, Goldman knew just about enough to win the approval of Judith Shklar, a severe examiner. He was awarded his doctorate with an overall grade entitling him to teach at Harvard. At the end of the exam, Shklar smiled and remarked that Merle Fainsod—another Harvard teacher, a leading analyst of Soviet politics and director of the Russian Research Center—had also been a mediocre in political theory as a doctoral candidate.

THE COMMUNIST EXPERIMENT

Let us return to Goldman's early days at Harvard. In his third and fourth years, Zbigniew Brzeziński became his academic advisor and another important companion. Like so many at the university, the Warsaw-born Brzeziński was a victim of the devastation which scourged Europe in the mid-twentieth century. In 1938, his father, a diplomat, was transferred to Montreal and appointed as Polish consul to Canada. Zbigniew's brother was seriously ill with polio and it was thought that the warm mineral springs in the town of Warm Springs, Georgia, might provide relief. Canada is considerably closer to Warm Springs than Poland.

The Brzezińskis did not return to their homeland. The family decided to stay in North America after Roosevelt, Churchill, and Stalin met at Yalta at the end of the war, reorganizing the European balance of power and putting Poland into the Soviet sphere of influence.

The family had already felt the impact of Stalin's terror, even before the war: the Brzezińskis had lived in the USSR for two years between 1936 and 1938, during the "Great Purges," when almost a thousand people a day were killed within the Soviet Empire because Stalin viewed them as political opponents or otherwise "unreliable." The experience left a deep impression on the Brzezińskis.

Like Henry Kissinger, Brzeziński was a representative of Harvard's realist school of international politics. According to this line of thought, every state is primarily interested in its own survival, striving to be more powerful than other states. Goldman was equally impressed by both professors; however, Brzeziński leaned toward the Democratic Party and Kissinger toward the Republicans, the two men often held opposing political views, and they did not get on well on a personal level. But perhaps precisely because of the polarity between the two men, Goldman himself became a master of dialectical reasoning.

Brzeziński worked at the Russian Research Center, which allowed Goldman to develop his growing interest in Eastern Europe. Here too, he met Merle Fainsod, the institute's famous director, who had been Brzeziński's teacher.

Fainsod was a regular advisor to US governments on the USSR, a particularly important subject during the Cold War.

In 1953 Fainsod published *How Russia Is Ruled*, then one of the best analyses of the development of Kremlin policy from Lenin to Stalin. In 1958, he published *Smolensk under Soviet Rule*, a book-length investigation into Stalinist rule in the Russian city of Smolensk in the years before the war. Fainsod's book is a shocking document of Stalin's absolute power, which confirmed the long-held suspicion that the Communist Party of the Soviet Union had been the dictator's willing helper, right down to smallest party organizations, which carried out Stalin's ideas and desires without having to be told.

In 1958, the same year which saw the publication of *Smolensk under Soviet Rule*, Guido Goldman and John Mudd traveled to the Soviet Union for six weeks as part of a group of forty students from various American universities. There were four sections within the group, each with ten participants. Mudd and Goldman were placed in a group called "Experiment in International Living," which had been founded by Mudd's mother.

This was the first time that students had made this kind of trip to the Soviet Union. But this was not a student "exchange," since the journey went in one direction only, eastward. Nor did the American students live with Russian host families: instead, they were put up in youth hotels and holiday camps. John Mudd kept a detailed diary of the trip.

Mudd and Goldman took a ship across the Atlantic, then traveled by train via Berlin and Brest in Belarus, eventually arriving in Moscow. Here, they were warmly welcomed and given bouquets of flowers. As was customary in the USSR, their hosts packed their days, putting on a dense program of political events. "Visits to factories, construction sites, educational institutions and 'informal' youth meetings," observed the young John Mudd in his diary.

The students were dragged through the main building of Moscow's Lomonosov University for several hours. When it was opened in 1953, the colossal building, constructed in the Stalinist confectionery style, was the tallest edifice in the world outside North America. Mudd wrote in his diary: "It is one of the most impressive achievements of the Soviet regime . . . and a work of great collective pride for Soviet citizens who have to endure cramped living conditions and meager consumer goods in their daily lives." Goldman and Mudd also visited the famous GUM department store, where they were amazed at long lines in front of shops containing almost nothing to buy.

The next leg of the journey was an overland drive to the Ukrainian capital Kiev. En route, they were astonished to see villages where the houses had no electricity or running water. In Kiev, the group was housed outdoors, on the banks of the Dnieper: every morning, they had to wash with river water. The hosts led their American visitors through a huge agricultural *kolkhoz*, then filled them so full of vodka that, as Mudd wrote, they had to be driven back in several cars, "because most of our group could no longer stand upright."

At this time, Ukraine formed part of the Soviet Union. The SS and German Wehrmacht had done terrible damage to the country during the war. Moreover, the wounds were still far from healed, as Mudd and Goldman repeatedly experienced en route. They also had learned about this part of the world from their Harvard studies: some Jewish emigrants studying or teaching at the university had been born in cities like Lviv or Chernivtsi, which were transferred to Ukraine after the war.

But the trip was also fun. The Americans taught the Russians to dance the Charleston, while in the evenings they watched Russian silent films or went for moonlit walks along the Dnieper. Every few days, as Mudd's diary reports, a "Soviet agitator" gave a political lecture on a subject like "US Imperialism in Lebanon." The students also made a detour to the Crimea, where they went swimming in the waters of the Black Sea.

Last but not least came Leningrad, which some three decades later would be restored to its original name of Saint Petersburg. Goldman and Mudd were impressed by the city on the Neva, for its architectural beauty and great wealth of European art, but also because Leningrad, as Mudd wrote, "offers many more opportunities to come into contact with interesting Soviets, mostly students. . . . In the streets and parks, it seemed extremely easy to find people who wanted to talk to us, often in a very frank way."

From Leningrad, the group took another short excursion, into the forests on the USSR's eastern border area. On the other side of the border was Finland, and the free western world, the system of values and order which Goldman would seek to defend by establishing several important institutions a decade and a half later.

For Goldman, in any case, the trip into the communist realm had a lasting effect. Back at Harvard, he decided to dedicate his senior thesis to a Soviet topic, to be written under the guidance of his mentor Brzeziński. "Zionism under Soviet Rule" was the title Goldman, not entirely unpretentiously, chose for his one-hundred-page bachelor's thesis, alluding to Fainsod's groundbreaking work, *Smolensk under Soviet Rule.*

In his research, Goldman learned that it was mainly Russian Zionists who created the first *kolkhozes* in the Soviet Union in the 1920s. The *kolkhozes* were a sort of agricultural commune, where the Zionists hoped to prepare for emigration to Palestine and the establishment of kibbutzes in the promised land.

But the Zionists soon became a thorn in the side of the communists. However, the Zionists' worst enemies were other Jews, members of the Yevsektsiya, a Jewish subgroup within the Communist Party. Founded with Lenin's support in 1918, the Yevsektsiya was convinced that Zionism and Jewish traditions stood in the way of the ideals of Soviet communism and must be fought with all severity.

The Yevsektsiya despised the Jewish bourgeoisie and the Hebrew language; it occupied synagogues and turned them into party offices. Zionism was declared a doctrinal threat to the state. In the end, in a great historical irony, the Yevsektsiya leaders themselves fell victim to the purges, imprisoned in camps or executed.

Zbigniew Brzeziński took a liking to Goldman's topic, not least since there was as yet hardly any literature on it. Goldman found sources in seven different languages, only three of which he could read himself—German, French, and English. Most sources were in Yiddish, so Goldman paid a translator. Brzeziński and the other examiners received Goldman's thesis enthusiastically, awarding it summa cum laude, the highest possible grade.

CHAPTER 5

Why Germany, of All Places?

THE OTHER WORLD

In the summer of 1959, Guido Goldman went to Germany for the first time in his life. More precisely, he went to the Federal Republic of Germany: West Germany. Having earned his bachelor's degree, he won a scholarship from the German Academic Exchange Service (DAAD) to study for one semester in Munich and one in Paris. He returned the scholarship money to the DAAD, believing it should be used to support less well-off students.

Of course, Munich was by no means Goldman's first contact with Germany. His parents had grown up there and were still very German in their instincts and outlook. At home on the Upper West Side, the Goldmanns were surrounded by German literature and music, as well as masterpieces of European art. The delicate Meissen porcelain was taken down when guests came to dine. For a time, a few years after the war, Nahum was living semi-permanently in Bonn while negotiating compensation for Holocaust survivors with with Konrad Adenauer, West Germany's first chancellor, with whom Nahum enjoyed a good relationship.

In 1959, traces of the war and the Holocaust were palpable everywhere, but these atrocities, although a ubiquitous presence in the Goldmann family, were not the only thing determining their image of Germany, nor did they define Guido Goldman's opinion of the country he was getting to know. When the Goldmanns spoke about Germany, they had the Germany from the decades before the Nazi era in mind. These were happy, beautiful, fulfilling years for them, which they looked back on with pleasure and pride, their view at times deeply tinged with nostalgia.

Avrom Udovitch, the Goldman brothers' close New York friend and a constant visitor to their home, says that, like so many German Jews, the Goldmanns from Frankfurt and the Gottschalks from Berlin suffered from a very particular trauma. "It broke their hearts that after Hitler came to power they were expelled and excluded from a society and culture that was also their society and their culture, which they loved, and which meant a great deal to them."

Germany, says Udovitch, bore very different memories for the Goldmanns than for his own family. For Udovitch's parents, who grew up in the humble surroundings of an Eastern European Jewish shtetl, everything German was taboo after the Holocaust. They had no positive associations with Germany from the time before the "Third Reich," because they simply did not know it. "The Shoah," he says, "wrapped Germany in deep, heavy black cloth, preventing anyone from casting the country in a good light, even to the least degree."

The Udovitchs emigrated to the plains of Canada long before the war, in the early twentieth century, taking their Orthodox beliefs and shtetl traditions with them. Yiddish was spoken at home, all the religious festivals were celebrated, and the Sabbath was strictly observed.

Udovitch will never forget how, shortly after the end of the war, at the age of thirteen, he drove with a rabbi from Winnipeg to Montreal to meet Auschwitz survivors at the airport. They were Hungarian Jews, could only speak Yiddish, and Udovitch, a student fluent in many languages, had the job of translating. His heart froze when people recounted the horrors of the camps. Udovitch himself lost his grandmother, an uncle, and other relatives in the Holocaust. "I only knew they were murdered because my father was weeping," he says. "My father never cried." For this reason, his family wanted nothing more to do with Germany or the Germans. "Even to *think* of buying a Volkswagen Beetle," says Udovitch, "would have betrayed the victims of the Holocaust." This was not the case for the Goldmanns, who retained many good and delightful memories, and themselves remained very German in many ways.

Goldman's friend Andrei Markovits also found it difficult to be reconciled with Germany, the country which had plunged Europe into a horrific war and carried out the industrially organized murder of millions of Jews, Sinti and Roma, homosexuals, people with disabilities, and opponents of the regime. For Markovits, Germany was not just the land of great poets and thinkers, but also the country of Hitler, Himmler, Eichmann, and Goebbels. His parents were Romanian Jews and after the war Markovits attended a strict Viennese high school, where the cane was used liberally and, as he says sarcastically, "Germanic discipline and order" prevailed.

Unlike Guido Goldman, Markovits would never have gone to Germany to study in 1959. He only made his peace with the country when the generation of 1968 took to the streets in rebellion against their parents. That process began when student leader Rudi Dutschke and the "extra-parliamentary opposition" confronted the former Nazis who, even after the war, occupied senior positions in government and administration, in universities, business, and justice. It continued in the 1980s, when the Greens entered city councils and parliaments for the first time, breaking taboos and shaking up Germany's ossified politics.

Markovits first came to West Germany in 1974, fifteen years after Goldman. "My Germany," he says, "was completely different from Guido's. It was rebellion, protest and alternative movements." The state loomed larger in the Germany to which Goldman arrived: the Germany of chancellors, presidents, and the postwar political parties, a world which Guido viewed partly through the eyes of his father Nahum.

MUNICH BLUES

As a doctoral student, Guido Goldman moved within his father's milieu, meeting Adenauer and Bertold Beitz, general manager of the Krupp Group. Thanks to Nahum Goldmann opening doors, his and his father's worlds inevitably overlapped.

Nonetheless, on this first visit to West Germany, Goldman had experiences of his own, and they were not always good ones. It was not love at first sight between Goldman and Germany, the country that later occupied such an important place in his life.

Compared to Harvard, the academic world at Munich University was hierarchical, traditional, and old-fashioned. When the young American student asked a professor for a reading list to go with his lecture, the German shook his head in disbelief and said: "That doesn't exist here. That is not provided!" Annoyed, Goldman wrote to his father: "Boy are the Germans ever order minded. It seems the philosophy common to all is, 'Ja, aber es muss seine rechte Ordnung haben' [Yes, but only in proper order]."

Goldman made hardly any friends in Munich, where his fellow students were more interested in parties and skiing than in studying, and the weather in autumn and winter is gray, damp, and depressing. "Somewhere deep down I think I wear a whopper of a resentment against this land and I suppose my attitude is: show me that it isn't justified," he wrote to John Mudd, while at the same time reassuring him that his low mood is only temporary.

In those days, Goldman was constantly drawn to the Seine, away from the Isar River that runs through Munich. In Paris he felt more comfortable, more at ease: his beloved aunt Ellen lived there, and Michael was also studying in the city. Nonetheless, he had no intention of abandoning the Munich experiment right away. "But I don't want to quit on Munich," he wrote to Mudd, "so I'll not depart before I do feel I've seen some good, solid, interesting times here."

Even if Goldman did not feel at home in Munich and found his course "far too lax," his mood was picking up. At first, he lived close to the main train station, but then rented a space in the fashionable Schwabing district, raving to his parents about his luxurious two-room apartment—with kitchen, bathroom, and balcony. In Paris he bought a second-hand Peugeot cabriolet, and drove it across the German countryside, in the mood for adventure.

At that time, many country roads and motorways had huge billboards showing the outline of the German Reich, encompassing Austria and the lands lost to Poland and Russia after the war, with the slogan: "Divided in three? Never!" The images were propaganda for the persistently revisionist "Kuratorium Unteilbares Deutschland" (Initiative for an Indivisible Germany), campaigning for the restoration of Germany's 1937 borders. They called for not only the unification of West and East Germany, that is, the Federal Republic and the German Democratic Republic (GDR), but also for the "recovery" of formerly German eastern territories which the four winning powers had assigned to Poland and the Soviet Union at the end of the war, including Pomerania, Silesia, and East Prussia.

Goldman and an American friend from Munich were outraged and wanted, as Goldman said, "to do something against this German revanchism." They printed out flyers with the words "Where's the Third Part?" and stuck them on top of the posters. Unfortunately, the police caught them doing it and imposed a fine.

Goldman also had another unpleasant rendezvous with the law in Germany when his mother came to visit him in Munich for a few days. Alice Goldmann had not returned to Germany since the early 1930s. She had arranged to meet her son for a cup of coffee at her hotel, the elegant Hotel Vier Jahreszeiten. As Goldman was reverse parking in front of the hotel, an acquaintance drove past and honked his horn. Goldman waved, lost attention for a second, and must have unknowingly nudged the bumper of the vehicle behind him. A guest in the hotel café saw the incident and immediately reported it to the police, saying nothing to Goldman. "I like Germany a lot," said Goldman, "but that was really typically German."

One way or another, two officers in green uniforms suddenly materialized at the table, brusquely ordering Goldman to come to the police station. Alice Goldmann felt as if she were back in Nazi Germany and seemed close to a nervous breakdown. The bumper was inspected, revealing a tiny scratch barely visible to the naked eye. But the police were adamant: "A scratch is a scratch: it's property damage."

At the police station, Goldman realized that he was not carrying his passport or his driver's license. The police wanted to keep him at the station until he produced some identification. Goldman told them that if they did not release him, he would not be able to produce the documents. This went back and forth in a catch-22 exchange. At one point, Goldman got annoyed and blurted out: "Now I can understand how Hitler and 1933 could happen."

The police were affronted by the statement. But, probably suspecting Goldman was a Jewish name and seeking to avoid further fuss, they dropped the "property damage" issue, but only on condition that he presented his passport and driver's license by five o'clock that afternoon.

Goldman left Munich for Paris in the spring of 1960 to spend his second European semester there before returning to Harvard in the summer. Back at his alma mater, he began postgraduate studies, which in theory would end with a doctorate. But Goldman was unsure of what to study, especially since he would need to find a topic to hold his attention for several years without boring him to tears. It was the old dilemma of this eternal seeker: torn between his many different interests, he could not make up his mind.

EXPEDITION TO AFRICA

When Goldman arrived at Harvard that summer, John Mudd was no longer around. He had gone to Berlin, where he was studying at the Free University on a scholarship. Goldman missed his friend and advisor a great deal. He repeatedly wrote to Mudd, long letters about his turmoil, his many disorganized thoughts, and the future plans buzzing around his head.

One letter in particular epitomizes Goldman's fickleness and volatility, but also the diversity of his interests. He writes that his father was considering becoming more politically active in Israel, maybe even running for office, so he wanted Guido to support him by spending more time in Israel. Maybe, says Goldman, this was not a bad idea.

In the very next line, however, he raves about studying at the renowned Institute for International Affairs in Geneva, combined with a project in Africa run by the International Labor Organization. But just moments later, he suggests maybe it would be wisest to go back to Russian studies, since he has some experience and a good advisor in Brzeziński. On the other hand, he says, since he already wrote a bachelor's thesis on a Soviet topic, he fears becoming overspecialized if he concentrates on Russia.

Then the letter switches to yet another completely new idea: in fact, his dearest wish is to return to Europe, he says, to learn more about its traditions and culture, get to know many more Europeans, and spend time exploring the continent's mountains and fabulous theaters. He would like to cycle across Europe on his bike, he adds, "to get a stimulating change of atmosphere from Harvard."

In the *next* paragraph, Goldman toys with a total break, saying he is considering transferring universities, maybe studying a while at MIT (Massachusetts Institute of Technology) in Boston to grapple with increasingly important economic issues. MIT, he writes enthusiastically, recently sent twelve students to Nigeria to help with the economy and industry. "Maybe it's time," he says, "to wing off for Africa or Nepal or Vietnam and something more exotic and starkly different, stimulating in entirely new ways."

In the summer of 1962, this eternally questing soul actually did travel to West and East Africa. However, Goldman did not go there to help stimulate the economy but to discover the extent of Soviet influence on the continent, in the company of Zbigniew Brzeziński and other staff from the Russian Research Center. There was growing concern in the United States about Moscow's attempt to spread communism in the Third World, and discussion about how best to keep it in check.

But the Harvard expeditionary force found nothing in any of the countries they examined. There was no evidence of Soviet influence in Ghana, Nigeria, Kenya, or Uganda. "We found nothing that would have been of concern to Americans in any way," says Goldman. They did see some odd things, but they had no relevance to the investigation. In Ghana, for example, where temperatures never come close to freezing, they saw several dozen Soviet tractors with snowplow equipment. Snowplows in Africa? At that time, Ghana urgently needed tractors for agriculture, but it seems Moscow only had Siberian models on offer.

DODGING A BULLET

Fears of growing Soviet influence were not unfounded. Goldman's expedition in search of African communism came at a very tense political time. On August 13, 1961, with Moscow's backing, members of East Germany's border police and army blocked road and rail routes into West Berlin and began building a wall across the city. A resolution of the ruling Council of Ministers stated that the new border arrangements were necessary "to stop the hostile activity of revanchist and militarist forces in West Germany and West Berlin."

One year later, in July 1962, the Soviet Union secretly began stationing Russian soldiers in Cuba, under the code name Operation Anadyr. Military bases were established, and for months, dozens of Russian ships transported military equipment to the Caribbean island, almost within sight of the coast of Florida. US reconnaissance aircraft revealed preparatory work for a launch pad for Soviet medium-range missiles.

This set off a nerve-wracking and highly dangerous tug-of-war between the two superpowers. In October 1962, President Kennedy imposed a sea blockade, but at the last minute Khrushchev, the Soviet leader, relented. War was averted, but tensions did not diminish, and there would be repeated bouts of saber rattling in subsequent years. Both the Americans and Russians continued to build up their armaments, each with their hand dangerously close to the nuclear trigger.

One consequence of this was increased American defense preparation, meaning more young men were drafted for military service. In 1962, the authorities turned their attention to Guido Goldman. As a student, he had previously benefited from a military service deferment, but the political situation meant he was now reclassified as Category 1-A. This would mean Goldman would have to serve if he was passed fit. As a healthy young man, well over six feet tall, there was little doubt he would be.

Goldman was deeply concerned and wrote to his father: although he had the right to object to the new classification, if the "1-A decision" was not overturned, "I could very well be inducted into the army by the end of September, since the build-up is taking place rapidly."

His only chance was Harvard. If a number of professors could vouch that he was indispensable to the academic life of the university, he would probably be downgraded to category 2-S, putting him at the back of the conscription line. The draft would be unlikely, for the moment at least.

Zbigniew Brzeziński, Merle Fainsod, and the political scientist Rupert Emerson backed Goldman. The draft committee changed its decision, Goldman was recategorized as 2-S and could breathe easy again. Later in life, he would say his own example demonstrated how the sons of wealthy, privileged families could evade military service. "Poor students and those without influential connections had no chance of deferment."

HENRY KISSINGER'S DECISIVE QUESTION

The trip to Africa brought no further enlightenment to Goldman about his future plans. In 1962, Goldman's intentions were no clearer: it would be a full year before he gained clarity. In late 1963 or early 1964, not long after the Kennedy assassination, Karl Kaiser, a young German political scientist, held a

Guido Goldman and Karl Kaiser in Bonn in 1983.

seminar at Lowell House at Harvard, speaking on the new significance of the Federal Republic. Goldman was so impressed that he immediately decided to dedicate his studies, specifically his PhD dissertation, to German topics. Later, Goldman said: "It had to happen that way, it was already in my biography and in my genes."

Kaiser was only three years older than Goldman and newly arrived at Harvard, having finished his dissertation at Nuffield College in Oxford. The college, founded in 1937 and specializing in sociology and political science, was one of the newer foundations in the almost thousand-year-old university. Meanwhile, Stanley Hoffmann, Goldman's former mentor, was causing a sensation at Harvard with *In Search of France*, a groundbreaking edited book, which offered new analysis and fresh interpretation of French politics and France's role in the world. Hoffmann's colleague Henry Kissinger wanted to carry out a similar study of Germany and needed a suitable assistant. Someone recommended Kaiser, the brilliant young scholar, then just twenty-nine years old.

At the time, Kissinger was the deputy director of the Institute for International Affairs and also ran the "International Seminar," which he had helped set up in the 1950s while still a student at the university. Every summer, the seminar brought together journalists, artists, writers, filmmakers, and politicians from all corners of the world. The communist bloc was not represented, because their citizens were either prevented from leaving by their own governments or were prevented from entering the United States by the staunchly anti-communist administration in Washington.

Most participants in the seminar were European or American. One was the journalist Theo Sommer, later editor-in-chief of the German weekly *Die Zeit*. Like both Goldman and his father Nahum, Kissinger had close connections to *Die Zeit*, especially to its publisher Marion Gräfin Dönhoff and Helmut Schmidt, who joined the paper's management after the end of his chancellorship in 1983. Kissinger even appeared at editorial conferences on a few occasions; he appreciated discussions with young journalists.

However, Kissinger relationship to *Die Zeit* was not without tension. It repeatedly published articles accusing him, as part of the US government, of supporting the coup against Chile's democratically elected socialist president Salvador Allende in September 1973. The US role in the Vietnam War was also heavily criticized. But Kissinger's friendship with Schmidt remained unaffected. When the former chancellor died in November 2015, the ninety-two-year-old

Kissinger flew to Germany and, leaning on a cane, gave a moving funeral speech at Hamburg's St. Michael's Church.

In the mid-sixties, when Kissinger was teaching at Harvard, thinking about *In Search of Germany*, West Germany was the focus of much attention in American politics. There was a lot going on in what was known as the "Bonn Republic": it was a time of upheavals and fresh starts. The Social Democrats were gaining support, and it seemed very likely that the party would soon hold the reins of power for the first time since the end of the Weimar Republic in 1933. This was viewed with concern on the other side of the Atlantic, not least by Kissinger.

Willy Brandt, Herbert Wehner, and Fritz Erler, leading Social Democrats at the time, were carefully shifting their party's course on foreign and security policy, and wanted to communicate their reliability and predictability to Washington. As a matter of national policy, the Social Democratic Party (SPD) would now support West Germany's close integration into the Western community of values and membership in NATO.

In the mid-1960s, Kissinger and his institute director Robert Bowie wanted to hear more about these political developments on the German left. They invited Erler to participate in a series of lectures at Harvard. Erler was passionate about foreign policy, spoke fluent English and, as chair of the parliamentary party, was an important figure within the SPD. An opponent of Hitler at a young age and a political prisoner between 1939 to 1945, he enjoyed an impeccable reputation in the United States, especially among Harvard professors who had escaped the Nazis.

Erler succeeded in establishing trust, including with Kissinger, who would soon go to work for the Nixon administration. Harvard published Erler's lectures in the summer of 1965; they also came out in West Germany, under the title *Democracy in Germany*. "This book was not written for the sake of the election campaign," wrote *Die Zeit* at the time, "It contains . . . the views of one of Germany's leading Social Democrats, but they are not framed as an attack . . . Rather, this is a detached, scholarly investigation of conditions in West Germany and the goals of his own party . . . In his final lecture, Erler tries to persuade the Americans to trust Germans in general, rather than any particular party. He argues confidently, without sentimentality or pandering, putting forward clear and plausible reasons." Late in 1965, Fritz Erler became seriously ill with cancer and died in February 1967.

Karl Kaiser once coined an excellent phrase: that for a long time West Germany had no foreign policy of its own, but foreign policy—Allied foreign policy—created the state of West Germany. During this period, almost everything was determined by the Allies, and the Bonn Republic could do little to shape its own foreign relations. Every unauthorized change in policy, every attempt at emancipation, such as Willy Brandt's new policy toward Eastern Europe in the early 1970s (known as *Ostpolitik*), was met with reservations and often with resistance.

But foreign views of West Germany gradually changed over the course of the sixties and seventies. The Nazi era and the Shoah did not disappear from public debate. How could they, considering the great weight of guilt hanging over the country? But the problematic German past was no longer the sole, immediate dominating factor in foreign public opinion. The *New York Times* stopped putting every unspeakable utterance from old Nazis on its front page.

Attention was now focused on the "German economic miracle" and the growing importance of West Germany in the escalating superpower confrontation between America and the Soviet Union. Along with this, western European countries were moving closer together on issues around future coexistence, self-defense, and Europe's role in the world. The Bonn Republic was at the heart of these new discussions, acting with new and increasing self-confidence. As Karl Kaiser puts it: "Suddenly America had to fight for Germany, and could no longer be absolutely certain that Bonn would always do exactly what Washington demanded."

In Harvard too, the 1960s were a time of upheaval and new beginnings. Several professors who had inspired academic interest in Europe and Germany were retiring or otherwise leaving the university. Kissinger made a political career in the Nixon administration; Kaiser was appointed to a professorship in West Germany, where he also acted as an adviser to Chancellor Brandt. There were no successors in sight and—unlike Russian studies, for example—there was no secure space, no institute of its own where scholarly interest in Europe could be focused. So there were fears that Germany and Europe, although increasingly important politically and economically, might become less relevant to academic life, and perhaps ultimately disappear completely.

This concern was shared by Goldman, still a doctoral student at the university, and newly enthused about Germany. He felt that Harvard unquestionably had to do something about this, for example by founding a "German Research

Program," an academic study program devoted to Germany. He discussed the idea with his close confidant Stanley Hoffmann. Although no friend of Germany, the historian thought the idea was good, advising Goldman to speak to Kissinger.

By now Kissinger was Goldman's doctoral supervisor. During the fall of 1966, Goldman invited his professor to lunch at the elegant faculty club and told him about his concerns and ideas. Kissinger listened politely, but, as Goldman later recalled, showed no particular interest, preferring instead to find out what was going on in Bonn. In West Germany, the Christian Democrat chancellor Ludwig Erhard was in power, but his government was in considerable difficulty. Erhard, Adenauer's successor, was widely felt to be a lame-duck chancellor, his days numbered.

In the 1965 election, Erhard had taken his party to another major victory, but once in power, the former minister for economic affairs, famous as the "father of the German economic miracle," had no luck. By 1966, the country was threatening to slide into recession, and Erhard's party, the Christian Democratic Union (CDU), had narrowly lost its majority in state elections in North Rhine-Westphalia, the largest state in the country and home to the key coal and steel industry. An increasing number of leading party allies began to distance themselves from the chancellor. Erhard's coalition partner at the federal level, the Free Democrats, were also increasingly nervous. Erhard's authority was rapidly eroding.

In view of all this, Henry Kissinger put the crucial question to his student: "Who will succeed Erhard?" Goldman went alphabetically through the Christian Democratic candidates, who were already restlessly jostling for position. When he arrived at Kurt Georg Kiesinger, the prime minister of the state of Baden-Württemberg, Kissinger interrupted: "Sure, it will be him, it will be Kiesinger." But Goldman objected: "Only if he passes the Nazi test."

When Kissinger frowned in response, Goldman informed him that Kiesinger had joined the Nazi party very early on, in February 1933. Working in the Reich Foreign Ministry, he advanced to become deputy head of broadcast policy, tasked with spreading Goebbels's propaganda. This fact, said Goldman, could possibly scupper Kiesinger's chances.

Kissinger was astonished, growling in disbelief that he had been completely unaware of this, although he was usually well-informed on political matters. The meal came to an end. The following day, the front page of the *New York Times* carried a report of Kiesinger's Nazi involvement. Shortly afterward,

Kissinger called Goldman, telling him: "I want a German Research Program and I will run it myself."

Goldman was delighted, saying he already had some ideas: the program could offer its own seminars, start research projects on the Federal Republic, and offer scholarships to bring German academics to Harvard. Kissinger asked Goldman to write down his thoughts and think about sources of money for the new venture.

Goldman was ideally suited for the job. If anyone could raise money on the back of a good idea, it was Goldman, who—thanks to his father—already enjoyed good connections with prominent figures in West Germany. He was a regular visitor to the country for his dissertation research. He had, for example, heard about Kiesinger's dark past from the diplomat Hans Otto Bräutigam, who, in 1966, was working under Gerhard Schröder, the Christian Democrat foreign minister, as a legation secretary at the German foreign office.

At the time, Schröder (not to be confused with the later Social Democratic chancellor of the same name) was also spoken of as a possible successor to Erhard. However, Kiesinger prevailed on the third ballot of the internal party vote. On December 1, 1966, he was elected chancellor with the combined votes of the Christian Democrats and Social Democrats, creating the country's first "grand coalition." Social Democrats joined the government for the first time since the Weimar Republic, with Willy Brandt appointed as foreign minister.

Goldman had also got to know Kurt Birrenbach, another CDU politician, through his father. Birrenbach was the chairman of the wealthy Thyssen Foundation, and Goldman was keen to win his backing for the German Research Program, including financial support. A lawyer and financial expert, Birrenbach had emigrated to Uruguay in 1939 to marry his girlfriend. She had been classified as "half-Jewish," and Nazi race laws made any marriage in Germany out of the question. Birrenbach had returned in the mid-1950s, and ever since had campaigned for good relations with the United States. In the 1960s, he became a member of the Atlantik Brücke ("Atlantic Bridge"), a non-profit set up to promote German-American understanding. Some years later, Goldman would become closely involved with its sister organization, the American Council on Germany. Birrenbach had the highest respect for Kissinger and liberally donated money for Goldman's research program.

Kissinger became director of the program, but in practice it was run by Goldman. At first, Kissinger had substantial doubts about Goldman's academic abilities. "I hardly noticed him in my seminars," said Kissinger years later, "so he can't have made much of an impression on me at first."

The subject of Goldman's dissertation was "the role of the German iron and coal industry after World War I." He had read that, in the 1920s, the steel and coal barons in the Rhine and the Ruhr—Germany's great industrial regions— had been far more afraid of being nationalized by the Social Democratic–led federal government of Germany than of being occupied by the French. So they tried to make life as difficult as possible for the government in Berlin, doing their best to boycott the reparations Germany was forced to pay after the losing World War I. As a result, French troops marched into the Rhineland, putting the industries out of Berlin's reach, much to the satisfaction of their owners and managers.

Goldman was fascinated by the episode: it was explosive historiographical information, little researched, but with a manageable amount of archival material. This suited Goldman well, since it meant the research would not monopolize his time, and he could continue with many other projects which were of equal or more importance to him.

A PLACEBO AGAINST THE KLAN

Goldman took his time with his dissertation, a lot of time. In early 1968, Kissinger asked him: "How long have you been in the doctoral program already?" At the time, the two were walking down Fifth Avenue, en route to the office of Nelson Rockefeller, the governor of New York, whom Kissinger was advising. Goldman told him the truth: "Nine years!" In response, Kissinger growled: "No graduate student of mine goes into double figures."

But Goldman was not wasting his time. As well as developing the German Research Program, he was also involved in the civil rights movement. During these years, he gradually came to recognize his purpose in life, beginning to chart his future course and the groundwork for his later political and philanthropic commitments.

The two dominant political themes of the era were the Vietnam war, where the United States was increasingly entangled, and the blatant injustice of racism. Of course Harvard was not untouched by the wave of protests.

In August 1963, hundreds of thousands of Americans marched on Washington in demonstration of equality, freedom, the right to work, and against the simmering war in Vietnam. Not far from the White House, in front of the Lincoln Memorial, Martin Luther King, Jr. gave his famous "I Have a Dream" speech. "I have a dream," he said, "that one day even the state of Mississippi, a state sweltering with the heat of injustice, sweltering with the heat of oppression, will be transformed into an oasis of freedom and justice. I have a dream that my four little children will one day live in a nation where they will not be judged by the color of their skin but by the content of their character."

One year later, President Lyndon Johnson, with King present, signed the Civil Rights Act into law. The following year saw the passing of the Voting Rights Act. Between them, these two laws asserted that Black Americans were equal citizens, and they ordered the desegregation of public institutions. However this did not by any means mark the end of racism. Day in and day out, the murder, beatings, arson, and discrimination continued.

Goldman and his friend John Mudd were horrified and were determined to do something to combat the problem. But how, and where? In New York, Goldman was a frequent visitor to the home of the judge Justine Wise Polier, a daughter of Stephen Wise, the great reforming rabbi and campaigner for equality and labor rights. In 1909, Stephen Wise cofounded the National Association for the Advancement of Colored People (NAACP), before being elected the first president of the World Jewish Congress in 1936. Thirteen years later, he would be succeeded in office by Nahum Goldmann.

Justine Wise Polier had inherited her father's courage and strong will. For decades, she had been fighting for the poor and for African Americans to have the same treatment in court as everyone else, becoming known as the "fighting judge." Through Polier, Goldman met Robert Moses, the Black civil rights activist and educator. Moses was an imposing personality, attractive and persuasive. A former Harvard student, he was among the most important civil rights organizers, coordinating nonviolent protests. In the southern state of Mississippi, which King's speech had singled out as an outstanding example of injustice, Moses was organizing a drive to register Black voters. In the United States, only those on the official electoral roll can exercise their right to vote.

Goldman was deeply impressed by Moses and introduced him to Mudd. Without further ado, he decided to pack his bags and join Moses's campaign in Mississippi. To protect himself from racists, he bought a German shepherd dog. The young Black lawyer Marian Wright had also gone to the South, where she courageously defended Black people in court. Wright was yet another friend of Goldman: a decade and a half later she would join the board of the German Marshall Fund, the transatlantic think tank set up by Goldman.

Before going to Mississippi to register voters, Goldman took a two-day preparatory course at Miami University, Ohio, in June 1964. On the course, volunteers were informed about the dangers of the work. Especially in the southern states, a commitment to civil rights could be a death sentence.

The seminar was chaired by Robert Coles, a thirty-five-year-old child psychiatrist, a teacher at Harvard, and a leading light in the civil rights movement. In 1960, he had accompanied Ruby Bridges for an entire year, giving support and advice to the six-year-old child and her family.

After the Supreme Court had ruled that racial segregation in public schools was unconstitutional, Bridges had become the first Black girl to attend the all-white William Frantz Elementary School in New Orleans. This was a huge and daunting challenge for a child her age, and indeed a life-threatening one. She had to be escorted to class by federal marshals, while white parents blocked her route to school, cursing and abusing her. One white mother threatened to poison her; another, snarling with hatred, showed her a small wooden coffin containing a black doll. US president Dwight Eisenhower ordered more marshals to New Orleans to protect her right to education.

At school, Bridges could eat only food she had brought from home. Both she and her parents were under tremendous pressure. Her father lost his job as a gas station attendant and the family was prevented from entering stores. Robert Coles provided the courageous family with psychological support, later basing his popular children's book *The Story of Ruby Bridges* about his experiences in New Orleans.

In the summer of 1964, as Coles was teaching volunteer voter registration workers about the risks involved, white racists from the Ku Klux Klan murdered three civil rights workers in Mississippi. The three, one Black and two white, were going door-to-door to add adult Black Americans to the electoral roll, close to the town of Meridian.

The killings prompted enormous shock across the United States. Robert Coles distributed tranquilizers to help contain rising panic among campaigners. However, as he later confirmed, the supposed tranquillizers were actually only placebos: Coles wanted to avoid any volunteer becoming dependent on pills. Some weeks later, Goldman was due to finally make his way to Mississippi.

Robert Moses was already on the spot, awaiting further support. But, just before he was supposed to leave, Goldman fell seriously ill with Pfeiffer's glandular fever, and was forced to stay at home. To the end of his life, he regretted not having been there.

Bob Moses, deeply frustrated by the lack of progress, gradually came to believe that whites were not good allies and Blacks should take things into their own hands. After moving to Africa for several years, he returned to the United States in the mid-1970s, where he devoted himself to the study of mathematics. When his daughter told him that her school did not teach algebra, he turned his attention to the teaching of mathematics in schools, setting up the "Algebra Project" to teach disadvantaged Black children.

A SUBVERSIVE READING LAMP

Once Goldman had recovered from his illness, he devoted more time to his doctorate. Between 1965 and 1969 he was a regular visitor to West Germany, often for months at a time. His father asked three people he knew well to make their archives available to his son: former chancellor Konrad Adenauer, Krupp manager Berthold Beitz, and Hermann Josef Abs, head of Deutsche Bank.

Adenauer said Guido Goldman was welcome to look at his documents, but they quickly proved irrelevant for his research into the machinations of the coal and steel barons. Through the bank's mediation, he interviewed Abs in a private compartment on a train from Bonn to Koblenz.

Beitz, the Krupp executive, proved the most important figure for Goldman's doctorate, inviting him to come to Essen to work with the Krupp archive in the Villa Hügel. "The huge collection of documents there," said Goldman, "was a gold mine for my research."

Goldman moved into a hotel in Essen for three months, driving every morning to the Villa Hügel, an imposing building in a vast park above Lake Baldeney. The Krupp von Bohlen and Halbach family, owners of the steel giant, had lived here until the end of World War II; of the building's two hundred and sixty-nine rooms, they used a mere one hundred and three.

After his months in Essen, Goldman went to Bonn, with the goal of exploring the political archive of the Foreign Office. There, as in Munich, he had experiences which might be described as "typically German," but these did not spoil his interest in and growing affection for the country.

Guido with Berthold Beitz (CEO of Krupp), on his seventieth birthday in Villa Hügel in Essen in 1983.

In Bad Godesberg, Goldman rented a room in a guesthouse which was also home to three members of the German parliament. Breakfast was always the same: two rolls for each person, along with a hard-boiled egg, butter, jam, and stomach-churning ersatz coffee, made from grain. Because Goldman tended to be in a hurry in the morning and preferred to buy real coffee en route to the library, he skipped breakfast. But one day his landlady brusquely informed him that he would have to leave. The three parliamentarians, it turned out, were fighting bitterly over his rolls, and two into three would not go. The landlady was determined to put an end to the disturbance. So as not to be shown the door, Goldman began putting the rolls in his pocket every morning.

The library of the Foreign Office was another place with strict rules. Here, the authoritarian tone and oppressive pedagogy of the Imperial and Nazi era was still alive and well. The archive was poorly lit, making it difficult for Goldman to make out the documents he was studying, even in daylight. As evening fell, reading became even harder. While there was ceiling lighting, this was not to be used, a rule enforced by a library attendant. Then when Goldman bought a small electric desk lamp, the guard ordered him to unplug the lamp immediately. "That electricity is paid for by the state!" the man barked.

Goldman, never at a loss for a solution, obtained a battery-operated lamp. The library guard couldn't object, but banished Goldman and his new device to the farthest corner of the archive. "I don't appreciate it," he said, standing in front of Goldman, "when one visitor has a lamp when other library users don't."

Goldman finally submitted his dissertation in 1969, receiving a very good grade. However, his research was never published: by now, he was very busy with other matters at Harvard, more important to him, above all, the establishment of an institution for the study of Germany and of Europe.

CHAPTER 6

Harvard
The Center for European Studies

A PLACE TO CALL HOME

In the 1950s and 1960s, the study of international politics at Harvard undoubtedly had its focus in the Center for International Affairs, later the Weatherhead Center. This was where Cold War conflicts were replayed and analyzed, with heated arguments about nuclear deterrence and the best defense policy for the West.

Here too, the great battles between the Gaullists and the Atlanticists took place, between those who thought Europeans should have closer ties to France and its independent nuclear deterrent, and those who felt it better to seek protection under the wing of the American eagle. In West Germany, the argument was fought out with particular passion in the conservative CDU and CSU parties.

The Center for International Affairs was unquestionably the leading institution for strategic studies in United States and worldwide, with the possible exception of the International Institute for Strategic Studies in London, founded in 1958. The *crème de la crème* of the transatlantic community met at the Harvard research center. Its director was Robert Bowie: a diplomat, a Republican and, from 1950 to 1952, legal advisor to John McCloy, US high commissioner in the recently established Federal Republic of Germany. Bowie's second in command at the institute was Henry Kissinger, a rising young academic star.

The world was becoming more and more complicated, with more diverse and confusing conflicts. Specialist knowledge of individual countries was increasingly a necessity. The clear trend in political science and the social sciences more generally was toward regional studies; half a century later, the opposite is true. At the same time, it was recognized that scholarship on international affairs should not become too narrow or one-sided. In a 1965 interview with the *Crimson*, Harvard's student newspaper, Stanley Hoffmann observed that political scientists should not come to the end of their studies clueless about Sigmund Freud or Max Weber.

Of course, the prevailing tendency toward regionalization and differentiation had an impact on the Center for International Affairs. As in the fission process of a nuclear explosion, its various elements began to separate into autonomous parts. New institutes emerged, covering disarmament, Russia, the Middle East, East Asia, Latin America, and ultimately also Europe and Germany.

However, mergers also took place. Two programs, the German Research Program and Kissinger's West European Seminar, came together to form an institution called West European Studies. Kissinger was not bothered by this development: at this point he was already looking beyond Harvard to Washington. But Robert Bowie went on the defensive, fearing for the future of the Center for International Affairs and keen to keep the subject of Europe exclusively within his institution.

On the faculty council, Stanley Hoffmann was a vigorous supporter of West European Studies, which would eventually become his academic home. Hoffmann was a major figure at Harvard, with a scholarly reputation extending far beyond the university. Students flocked to his lectures. Hoffmann's views carried weight and the faculty council approved his proposal. So as not to fully alienate Bowie, however, the name "Institute" was dropped, replaced with "Studies." West European Studies, it was agreed, obviously sounded comparatively harmless. In the 1970s, the name was changed again, to the Center for European Studies, CES for short.

To get the ball rolling, Kissinger installed his colleague Abby Collins at Goldman's side. Over the next decades, Collins would prove an important supporter of Goldman's efforts. Collins had already been running Kissinger's "International Seminar" for many years at the Center for International Affairs and she now provided Goldman with an office, up under the roof on an attic floor.

Just one year later, West European Studies moved into its own small building at 471 Broadway in Cambridge, directly across from Broadway Market, very close to the Harvard campus. The first German scholars were invited using German Research Program money, donated by the Thyssen Foundation. Joe Joffe, a political scientist, and later a newspaperman, was the first invitee; he ended up staying for four years. He was followed, among others, by the lawyer and contemporary historian Arnulf Baring.

Goldman also managed to get several million deutsche marks from other German firms and the federal government. He made one particularly smart, far-sighted and significant move, incorporating the John F. Kennedy Scholarship, in existence at Harvard since 1967, into his new institute. The program enabled young German scholars to study at the university for a year; once West European Studies was established, the new institute became their anchor. The John F. Kennedy Scholarship is a coveted award: its endowment has increased more than twentyfold over the decades, from $656,000 in its early days to over $15 million today.

The scholars in the program were selected in cooperation with the DAAD (the German Academic Exchange Service). In the late 1960s and early 1970s, they included many well-known German scholars, including the political scientists Sabine Müller von Levetzow and Manfred Knapp, historian Heinrich August Winkler, sociologist Wolfgang Zapf, and social historian Jürgen Kocka: a genuine who's who of cutting-edge academics researching West Germany.

Half a century later, long after the Berlin Wall fell, then German foreign minister Frank-Walter Steinmeier was asked to open the German scholarship to other Europeans, since Eastern Europeans in particular had virtually no chance of winning grants to study. Steinmeier was in favor, and the scholarship program was expanded. Since then, early career scholars from all over Europe have been able to study at Harvard. They are now referred to as German Kennedy Fellows.

Another indication of the changes that fifty years have brought is that in 2020, the current director of the Center for European Studies is Grzegorz Ekiert, a Polish-born political scientist with research interests on a particularly pressing contemporary topic: the future of democracy and the development of social movements and civil society, especially in Eastern Europe.

A DIVISION OF LABOR

To return to the earliest days of West European Studies: the new institute, although it could not officially use the term "institute," quickly became an attraction, particularly for the transatlantic elite, but also for ordinary students with an interest in Europe. Hoffmann and Goldman offered a joint seminar which was a magnet for students; their course on European systems of government was always fully booked. "Mainly because of Stanley," Goldman would say.

Hoffmann was a captivating lecturer, a never-ending fount of knowledge. Goldman, says Abby Collins, was more reserved, speaking quite softly, sometimes mumbling, so much so that at some point a microphone was attached to his lapel.

At the start of every academic year, the *Harvard Crimson* published an unofficial evaluation of professors. Goldman grinned at what this "Confy Guide" said about Hoffmann and him after the first year of their course: "A course you shouldn't miss: it takes you on a journey through very different topics. Hoffmann is a gifted teacher, and every student of politics should attend at least one lecture by him. Goldman also knows his stuff, but avoid the first few hours with him, they are a 'snooze cruise.'"

He went too easy on students back then, Goldman recalled, laughing. The course syllabus described in detail what he would cover at the beginning. "Everyone knew about that, so they could safely take a nap."

Guido Goldman taught at Harvard for a quarter of a century in all, from 1969 to 1994, but teaching always remained his secondary occupation. He had a doctorate and a teaching job, and he was founder and director of a university institute. It seemed like he had everything needed for a stellar scholarly career. But although well-respected colleagues thought Goldman had what it took to be an academic, he himself disagreed, and probably rightly.

Goldman did not like to stay long on one topic and had published little, nothing of major significance. His BA thesis "Zionism Under Soviet Rule" had been published in 1960 by the Theodor Herzl Foundation in New York. In 1974, Random House published *The German Political System*, a short guide to the government, constitution, and economy of the Federal Republic of Germany.

Goldman was well read, bright, entertaining, and funny. He could tell anecdotes nonstop and was enormously knowledgeable. But he remained an academic flaneur, a clever mind who left behind a great institutional legacy, but not an intellectual one.

Goldman lacked the patience and the interest to bury himself in libraries for months or years, working away at one academic topic. He was also fond of the good life and comfort to be found in New York and the city's intellectual salons, as well as his ability to shuttle back and forth between America and Europe. All of this would have been unaffordable on a professor's salary.

In fact, he earned his living by managing large fortunes: for many years, he served as head of the investment house First Spring. His friend Morris Offit, a successful New York money manager, says "Goldman could have been a really good investment banker, maybe one of the best." But to work only to increase others' wealth—and his own—would have kept him away from exciting, albeit time-consuming work at Harvard. This was certainly not what Goldman wanted. Goldman was, as Joe Joffe puts it, the best banker among Harvard academics and the best academic among New York bankers.

Leadership roles at West European Studies were established from early on: Stanley Hoffmann was the academic figurehead and intellectual driving force; Goldman was the impresario, institution builder, string puller, organizer, architect, and debt collector, in his own way he was just as brilliant as Hoffmann. Or, to put it differently, Hoffmann was a widely admired intellectual guru, for whom Goldman created a large, brightly lit theatre: the Center for European Studies.

Their joint success was possible only because they benefited from the trend toward small, autonomous university institutes. "We couldn't do it again today," said Goldman, with both realism and slightly wistfulness. Regional studies are now outdated, "completely out." Whether you research Norway, Poland, Belgium, or Italy, everything is crammed together into a single, large whole. "Scholarly rigor, including in political science," said Goldman, is now regarded as valid only "if topics can be quantified, put into figures, expressed in numbers and comparative statistics."

When West European Studies came into being in 1969, there was something fundamentally different at stake: spurring scholarly curiosity about Europe in America, and vice versa.

Given the ongoing political crises—and thanks to grants made available—this cross-fertilization took place quite quickly. Soon the building on Broadway became too cramped. West European Studies had long since become a sought-after place for young academics at Harvard. The historian Charles Maier and the political scientist Peter Hall, both working at the Center and both of whom would head the institute decades later, urgently needed an office to work in. There was also no library as yet and no reading room where young scholars could meet and discuss God and the world over a cup of coffee or a glass of wine. These things are exactly what make or break academic exchange.

Goldman went in search of something appropriate, quickly spotting a building at 5 Bryant Street, very close to the university campus, which at the time housed the Hillel Association. Named after a Jewish scribe, Hillel was then the world's largest Jewish student organization. But the organization was under financial pressure and needed to move premises.

The building was exactly the size Goldman had in mind. But where, and how, could he obtain money for rent and the necessary renovations? The Ford Foundation gave the institute a grant of $250,000 to cover three years, but without the possibility of renewal. The foundation had already announced it would no longer fund regional studies.

Goldman raised tens of thousands of dollars from wealthy friends, mostly from Marietta Sackler and Georges and Lois de Ménil. Goldman often went to New York for the weekend, where he kept a small apartment in Manhattan and went to receptions, openings, premieres, dinner parties. His social life increasingly gravitated to wealthy circles, where Goldman spanned a web of organizational connections, gradually expanding his network, the source of the multimillion-dollar capital for all his ventures. Goldman became friends with many people in this network, giving them gifts, sending flowers, offering advice in difficult situations, and later on, inviting them up to his Maine property on Vinalhaven. His unique cultivation of personal relationships also formed a considerable part of his success.

Marietta Sackler is one good example. The divorced wife of the Jewish entrepreneur Arthur Sackler—a psychiatrist who made tens of millions selling medicines, especially Valium—she was a good friend of Goldman and a regular donor to the institute at Harvard. Born as Marietta Lutze in pre–World War II Berlin she was rich in her own right as the owner of the German pharmaceutical company Dr. Kade. Like Goldman, she had a passionate interest in developments in Germany. Sackler lived for many years on Goldman's property in Concord, in a house directly across from him.

In the United States today, the name Sackler has a heavily tarnished reputation. But Arthur Sackler himself bears no blame for this. After his death, his two younger brothers founded Purdue Pharma, the drug company that made enormous amounts of money in the 1990s selling Oxycontin, a highly addictive pain reliever. The drug is now believed to have been the main cause of the terrible opioid epidemic which has ravaged whole areas of the country, particularly the Appalachians and Midwest. According to US health authorities, around seventy thousand people died in 2017 from drug overdoses, two-thirds of them from opioids like Oxycontin.

The political scientist Lois Pattison de Ménil, another patron of West European Studies, knew Goldman from her days as a student at Harvard, where she also studied with both Kissinger and Hoffmann. Her husband, Georges de

Ménil is an American economist of French descent who taught at Princeton and Sciences Po in Paris. Georges de Ménil's mother was the daughter of Conrad Schlumberger, the billionaire founder of the world's largest oil and gas exploration company, and she inherited his fortune.

But contributions from friends were not enough to restore the desired building at 5 Bryant Street to decent condition. The Hillel students who met there to eat kosher had left it in very poor shape. However, Goldman managed to persuade Irving Rabb, a Jewish businessman, to chip in a small amount for renovation work. Rabb ran Stop & Shop, a thriving Boston supermarket chain, and was an important sponsor of the student association. Goldman filled the last funding gap with his own money.

MOVING INTO THE "GERMANIC MUSEUM"

In 1970, West European Studies finally moved to 5 Bryant Street, where it would stay for almost twenty years until, in the fall of 1989, long since renamed the Center for European Studies, it moved to the historic Adolphus Busch Hall at 27 Kirkland Street, one of the grandest buildings in Harvard, formerly the Germanic Museum.

It is worth recounting the details of this coup. The story illustrates well the long and turbulent history of German-American relations, but it also serves as a particularly vivid illustration of Goldman's restless energy, shrewdness, ingenuity, and entrepreneurial talent. Whenever he took on a project, things unfolded in a similar pattern: first, he had a fixed idea, he would become increasingly infatuated with it, and then would work tirelessly, leaving no stone unturned until the idea became reality.

Adolphus Busch Hall, where the Center for European Studies is still located today, epitomizes a difficult chapter in German American history. In the late nineteenth century, three Harvard professors of German literature published an essay entitled "The Need for a Germanic Museum." They had been informed that the German Emperor might be inclined to bequeath some German art treasures to America. They moved quickly, fearing that cities like St. Louis or Milwaukee, which had large populations of German immigrants, might be preferred.

Their proposal fell on fertile ground, and Emperor Wilhelm II donated a large number of plaster casts of church monuments, initially shown at the

Adolphus Busch Hall.

Rogers Gymnasium in Harvard. Placed in that context, the monuments seemed so bizarre that, having toured the exhibit, the well-known philosopher William James wrote a light-hearted satire about the display.

But the temporary exhibition space in the gymnasium was soon entirely filled to capacity, so Harvard began to solicit money from wealthy German Americans to build a new home for the exhibition and to purchase more artworks to go with it. The request went almost entirely unheeded, except for Hugo Reisinger from St. Louis, Missouri, the son-in-law of the German American millionaire Adolphus Busch, whom he convinced to finance the museum.

Busch was the son of a hops trader from Kastel, near Mainz in Germany. In the mid-nineteenth century, he had emigrated to America, where he founded

Celebration of the CES move into Adolphus Busch Hall with Guido, Stanley Hofffmann, Charles Maier, and Abby Collins.

the Anheuser-Busch brewing company, earning him huge amounts of money. Ever since, the family has remained active as philanthropists and art collectors.

Thanks to Busch and Reisinger, Harvard could now build a museum. German Bestelmeyer, a Nuremberg-based architect, was commissioned to come up with a design. At that time, Bestelmeyer was one of the busiest architects in Germany, with projects including the expansion of Munich University.

Busch always spent his summers in his castle in Germany, and was wildly enthusiastic about Bestelmeyer's style, whose architecture has been described as having close connections to "southern German traditions," based on "traditional monumental conventions." Architectural forms from previous centuries, ranging from church buildings to Italian Baroque palaces, were a particular inspiration to Bestelmeyer. Aldolphus Busch Hall contains a mishmash of Romanesque, Gothic, and Baroque styles.

But the Germanic Museum had to wait still longer. The property chosen by Aldolphus Busch had a tenant, a Harvard professor who had no desire to move out, with a lease running until 1914. By the time the foundations could finally be excavated, Busch and Reisinger were both dead. Then World War I broke out, with Bestelmeyer serving in the German armed forces, so that the head of the Harvard architecture faculty, of all people, had to supervise work on the museum. He was English, meaning that his home country, during his oversight of the building work, was already at war with Germany.

Only in 1921 did the Germanic Museum finally open in Adolphus Busch Hall, with several German Jewish emigrants now among its major sponsors. Moreover, the collection was constantly expanding; in the 1930s, the then director, Charles Kuhn, bought a number of modern works outlawed by the Nazis as "degenerate art," prohibited from exhibition in Germany.

The museum was forced to close during the World War II, ultimately reopening in 1948. Because the name "Germanic" was by then no longer appropriate, Harvard renamed the museum in February 1950, giving it a slightly more unexceptional title: the Busch-Reisinger Museum of Germanic Culture. The collection grew ever larger: it is now the second largest collection of German and German American art in the United States, including large numbers of works by well-known painters such as Lyonel Feininger and Max Beckmann.

In the 1980s, however, it was revealed that many treasures of the Adolphus Busch Hall could no longer be properly stored. The installation of much-needed air conditioning in the old walls was technically difficult and unaffordable. A plan was drawn up to donate particularly sensitive works to the Fogg Museum at Harvard. So it was a good thing that Arthur Sackler, the pharmaceutical entrepreneur, left part of his extensive collection of Chinese art to the university in the 1970s. He was building his own museum right next to the Fogg building.

The question remained: what would become of Alphonsus Busch Hall when it was no longer a museum? When Goldman got wind of university plans to turn the building into offices, he told the faculty leadership this would be a serious misappropriation, verging on sacrilege. The Busch-Reisinger family wanted to use the museum to promote German culture, and a rededication would violate their intention, and would not stand up in court.

Goldman would not be Goldman if he did not already have an idea for an appropriate use of the old building. What would be more in keeping with the founders' request, he argued in front of the assembled faculty, than turning the former Germanic Museum into a place of study for German and European scholars, in short: to use it to host the Center for European Studies?

Harvard agreed. Goldman once more got out his Rolodex, mobilizing his contacts. The Hamburg entrepreneur Werner Otto, whose son Alex studied at Harvard, donated three million deutsche marks to the Fogg Museum to build an extension to house the Busch-Reisinger collection, which finally opened in September 1991. A new association, the Friends of the Busch-Reisinger Museum, paid for running costs; its members included the German industrialist Arend Oetker. Minda de Gunzburg's heirs chipped in another $15 million to renovate Adolphus Busch Hall, now renamed the Minda de Gunzburg Center for European Studies.

Baroness Aileen Mindel "Minda" Bronfman de Gunzburg.

Harvard President Derek C. Bok with Baron Alain de Gunzburg.

The de Gunzburgs, with their close connections to Harvard, were also important members of Goldman's network. Alain de Gunzburg had studied at the university and his son Jean, usefully enough, was a research assistant at the Center for European Studies in 1987, leading the research project "Comparative Science Policies in France and the United States." Minda de Gunzburg, the wife of Alain de Gunzburg, died in 1985, but her memory was preserved in the name of the new institution. Also a good friend of Goldman, she was the son of Samuel Bronfman, the founder of Seagram and a good friend of Nahum Goldmann, and the brother of Edgar Bronfman, the man who offered his private plane to fly Nahum Goldmann's body back to Israel. Guido Goldman has also been managing part of the de Gunzburg family assets since the 1980s and had close ties with Minda de Gunzburg's son Charles. Once again, the cogs meshed perfectly.

Guido with Charles de Gunzburg.

There would eventually be room for all of the Center's staff and students at the revamped Adolphus Busch Hall: professors and employees, doctoral and postdoctoral students. The institute's new home had seminar rooms, a library, and a large central hall where people come together on Fridays to have a snack and swap academic ideas and gossip. The hallways and sweeping stairwells showcase works of art that Goldman had donated to the CES from his private collection, including large paintings by Bernard Schultze, a German postwar modernist, and smaller works by Ida Kerkovius, an important exponent of twentieth-century modernism.

Even when it was still named West European Studies, located in a building on Bryant Street, the CES was very European in its thinking, style, and tone, with sophisticated lunches and dinners: an upscale meeting place for European academics and Americans who were enthusiastic about Europe. "With its hospitality and elegance," explains Josef Joffe, "the Center stood out from the rest at an early stage. Here, you were among your own kind, *entre nous*, and its presence served to civilize other university institutions."

The CES was no ordinary university institute. It soon enjoyed a stellar international reputation. In September 1989, EU Commission president Jacques Delors spoke at the formal opening of what would now be called the Minda de Gunzburg Center for European Studies, with a piano concert in the hall, and lavish food and drinks. "Dear Guido," wrote Baron Alain de Gunzburg enthusiastically from Paris, "the center is an immense success and I am very grateful for everything that you have created in memory of Minda."

Stanley Hoffmann was also fulsome in his praise for his new workplace at Adolphus Busch Hall, now looking splendid after its renovation: "Dear Guido," he wrote, "I really want to congratulate and thank you for all you've done for the flourishing of CES—the Busch is your Parthenon, and we are all in your debt. You've had the vision, skill, energy and wisdom to see it through. It's a splendid building. Onward to more and better things—with younger people coming on board."

Hoffmann was absolutely delighted with the new center, but he had one small wish: French doors to the garden to keep out the noise from outside. "I hope you'll support me: it's my only demand!" Hoffmann's wish was fulfilled, and he kept his spacious, ground-level office, with direct access to the vine-covered inner courtyard until his death in September 2015. This place always reminded him of France, his emotional home, he enthused when we met in the fall of 2006, adding with his characteristic smiling irony: "At least . . . if it weren't for the replica of the Brunswick Lion right in the middle."

The historian Charles Maier, who succeeded Goldman as the director of the institute, was given a large corner office in Adolphus Busch Hall, where he could shelve his thousands of books from floor to ceiling. Peter Hall, the political scientist who ran the CES from 2001 to 2006, was based in a roof-space office, while the current boss Grzegorz Ekiert has his workspace on the second floor. A room was also reserved for Guido Goldman, who founded the institute in 1969, kept it alive, and served as its director for a quarter of a century. Whenever he came by the building, which was not so often in the final years of his life, a desk was cleared for him.

VIETNAM AGAIN AND AGAIN

Over the years, academics, parliamentarians, executives, prime ministers, and presidents have come together at the Center for European Studies, first on Bryant Street, later on Kirkland. Chancellors Willy Brandt, Helmut Kohl, and Angela Merkel have held discussions with students here. Oskar Lafontaine, a prominent German politician who was then a Social Democrat, had a chauffeur drive him up to the CES in a massive limousine, but was angry that the seminar room could fit only one hundred people, who turned out to be primarily Europeans, not Americans, to his chagrin. Perhaps he did not understand he was visiting an institute for European Studies.

Whenever transatlantic relations have hit a rocky patch, the CES has been at the center of debate. The tireless scholarship holders are the main contributors to the academic life of the Center. While many professors prefer to hide behind their scholarship, these young academics from Europe and the United States seek out vigorous political debate. There were plenty of occasions for this in the seventies, eighties, and nineties.

The former CES librarian, Leonie Gordon, says that in 1972, in the midst of the Cold War, the legendary chess duel between the American player Bobby Fischer and the Russian Boris Spassky was re-enacted night after night in the reading room. People repeatedly ended up at loggerheads, albeit mostly amicably, she recalls, about the East-West conflict, about nuclear weapons, and about Brandt's *Ostpolitik*.

Some, including Karl Kaiser, felt at the time that German reunification should not be the be-all and end-all of relations with the Soviets. Instead, common ground should be sought, for the sake of peace and shared interests with the Kremlin. "Change through rapprochement" was Kaiser's motto, although some Americans, such as John McCloy, previously the US high commissioner to West Germany, believed this policy had been refuted by Warsaw Pact troops marching into Czechoslovakia in 1968. Brzeziński, who by now was teaching at Columbia and who would soon become National Security Advisor to President Jimmy Carter, had an entirely different strategy. Despite the crackdown on the Prague Spring, he continued to pin his hopes on reformist states in Eastern Europe, hoping at some point to surround the USSR with a ring of semi-democratic states.

Vietnam was another major issue at the CES. Stanley Hoffmann was a bitter opponent of the war, as shown by his legendary correspondence with

McGeorge Bundy, an advocate of US intervention in Vietnam, Kennedy's security advisor, and formerly a dean at Harvard. When Hoffmann, in one of the letters, reminds him of the French experience as the colonial power in Indochina, Bundy writes: "We are not the French—we are coming as liberators, not colonialists." Hoffmann replies: "The only problem was the Vietnamese," suggesting that American foreign policy tended to repeat the same mistakes over and over, committing "the sin of excessive benevolence: we want to make people happy, whether they want it or not." Time and again in US foreign policy, interventionism and isolationism have alternated, not least in 2020, at the time of writing, when the US once more seems bent on isolation, thanks to Donald Trump's America First policy.

Goldman's former colleague Abby Collins remembers that some CES scholarship recipients participated in sit-ins and lecture boycotts to protest against the Nixon administration's bombing of Cambodia. At Harvard, the students' anger about the war, says Collins, was particularly focused on Kissinger, the former director of the German Research Program and Bundy's successor as national security advisor.

Stanley Hoffmann was a friend of Kissinger's and felt very much torn. At the height of the antiwar mobilization, he spoke to the assembled student body, making the case for peace, both in Asia and on campus. However, he did not join the dozen or so professors who set out for the White House to protest the war, and their former colleague, in a very personal way.

To this day, Kissinger—who inherited the war rather than starting it, then expanded it before finally bringing it to a close—responds to criticism by saying opponents oversimplified things in their scathing criticism of US military intervention. "Our commitment," he said in October 2019, in a conversation in his apartment overlooking the East River in New York, "was not, as some believe, a product of evil, but rather the result of highly complex global political problems in the East-West conflict, more complex and more difficult than anything the United States had experienced so far." Unfortunately, he added, younger generations were often quick to make moral judgments, whereas "in politics, moral questions have complex origins and different, often ambiguous references."

One way or another, moral questions played a major role in debates at the Center for European Studies. People were unwilling to go along with "Kissinger's Realpolitik," with its ostensible or actual necessities, not least since history had shown that concept to be a deeply political one, astonishingly flexible and adaptable. Reality is not an immutable truth, permanently carved in stone. It can be viewed from different perspectives and interpreted in quite different ways.

The CES was not at all just about America. It also, repeatedly and with great intensity, addressed sensitive topics in both Europe and Germany. In the 1970s, the terror campaign of the Red Army Faction (RAF) in Germany cast its long shadow all the way to Harvard. Debates on structural violence and legitimate resistance were not new: they had been present at the university at least since the emergence of Latin American liberation movements. But this seemed a different question: the coming of left-wing terrorism seeking to violently overthrow the state and its representatives in West Germany, a democracy with a social market economy.

In 1970, the magazine *Agit 883* published its appeal "Assemble the Red Army," and a year later the RAF put out its strategy paper "The Urban Guerrilla Concept." The left-wing terror group carried out dozens of murders, arson attacks, bombing, airline hijackings, and kidnappings of politicians and industrialists. The "German Autumn" of 1977 marked the terrible climax of the violence.

Helmut Schmidt, the Social Democratic chancellor—who two years later, in 1979, would speak to Harvard graduates and visit the Center for European Studies—was bitterly opposed to the RAF campaign. His government passed a series of drastic antiterror laws, meeting with vehement criticism from liberals and leftists in both West Germany and the United States.

During one CES discussion of the new German police and legal measures, Claus Offe, a German sociologist, warned against a return of German fascism. Karl Kaiser, at the time a foreign policy adviser to the Schmidt government on foreign policy, reacted vehemently. Red-faced with anger, recalls Abby Collins, he described Offe's claims as "pure nonsense" and "foul accusations." Kaiser himself says Offe at the time was agitating against the German government in a "completely unscholarly" way, "in the style of the extra-parliamentary opposition."

At one and the same time, the Center for European Studies was and remains a battlefield, a seismograph, and a heart monitor. As Andrei Markovits—who led the heated discussion in which Offe made his provocative statements—puts it: it was a mirror of the zeitgeist. The debates could be great fun too, since the CES often served as a kind of academic avant-garde, displaying a keen sense for emerging social changes.

However, at times the CES lagged badly behind events. It took a very long time before the first German Greens were invited to Harvard. Considered the black sheep of German politics, they were held carefully at arm's length. Like almost all observers, the CES did not understand what was going on in East Germany in 1989 until late in the process, failing to appreciate the tremendous earthquake that the opposition "Monday demonstrations" had triggered.

James Bindenagel, an American diplomat and political scientist, and another friend of Goldman, who watched both the rise of the Greens and the fall of the wall, the end of the GDR, says it took time for the penny to drop in the United States. Bindenagel, until recently the Henry Kissinger Professor at Bonn University, was thirty at the time. He was working at the American consulate in Bremen when, in October 1979, the Green Party in Bremen crossed the legally required "five percent" threshold—parties need to achieve this level of votes to enter federal or state parliaments—and was elected to the parliament of the city-state.

Major figures joined the newly electable party: former radical student leader Rudi Dutschke, peace activist Petra Kelly, and Otto Schily, defense lawyer for the RAF who later became Minister of the Interior. "I felt a new political movement was emerging," says Bindenagel, "but no one in America was really interested. If they were, it was only because of the constant fear of new forms of German radicalization."

Bindenagel is a walking encyclopedia of German-American conflicts since the World War II: he can list them off at the drop of a hat, from Afghanistan and Iraq to cost-sharing in NATO. At least since the Carter presidency, American presidents have complained regularly that Germany owed its economic miracle to exports alone, spending too little on domestic consumption. At one time or another, Reagan, Bush senior, and Obama all called for the Federal Republic to increase defense spending.

A LARGE PURPLE PATCH

Guido Goldman was director of the Center during these turbulent years, but his office—first on Broadway, then Bryant Street, finally in Adolphus Busch Hall—was often of lesser relevance. He frequently donated wine and pizza for discussions between the fellows and staff at the Center, and was delighted with lively argument at the CES, but he himself kept his distance from debates. He felt that, as head of the institute in troubled times, he should maintain political restraint as much as possible. As a fundraiser, he also needed to maintain good relationships with all parties. Without donations, there would be nothing.

In private life, Goldman took a clear political stance, calling himself a "progressive moderate," located "radically in the political center." From the very start, Goldman was committed to human rights and civil liberties, and was an advocate of immigration and a supporter of Germany's social market economy. But he was disgusted by ideologues and ideologies of any kind, a stance to which dozens of letters to his friend Stanley Hoffmann can attest.

Hoffmann and Goldman traveled a great deal and, in their letters, regularly discussed the issues that motivated them, in personal matters, but above all politically. Time and again, their discussion returned to Vietnam. As early as the 1960s, under Kennedy and Johnson, Hoffmann and Goldman had somber forebodings of the entangled trap into which America was walking. "We are in a hopeless trap," wrote Hoffmann. Goldman agreed.

Goldman often went to Germany, maintaining contacts in politics and business and raising money for the chronically hard-up CES. A thousand other things also took up his time. When Kissinger joined the Nixon administration, Goldman helped him make the move to Washington, organized dinner parties for many years, and spent time with Kissinger almost every weekend. The new National Security Advisor could stay in Goldman's two-room New York apartment whenever he wanted. Perched on Goldman's living room couch, his bodyguards took care that no one climbed through the window. Kissinger often took advantage of Goldman's hospitality: New York was where his new partner Nancy Maginnes lived, whom he married in 1974.

Not all Nixon administration staff were sympathetic to Kissinger. There was considerable jealousy and internal spats. Among Nixon's close associates in particular, said Goldman, some "hated the German Jew from Harvard" and were determined to make life difficult for him. Kissinger often felt alienated and alone, and he needed a friend he knew he could trust absolutely. Goldman became his close companion.

The Kissinger-Goldman friendship sometimes became political, inevitably if German-American relations were involved. While Brandt and Schmidt were in power, whenever Goldman returned from Bonn, Kissinger would immediately bring him to the White House to pick his brains. Goldman's excellent contacts among Social Democrats meant he was a first-rate resource for Kissinger during his time as National Security Advisor and later as Secretary of State.

As a rule, however, the two spoke about everyday life: food, apartments, and mutual friends. When Kissinger needed a new reading lamp, Goldman went out and located one somewhere in the White House. He also lent Kissinger a painting from his art collection for his office, an abstract canvas with a large purple patch and black dots at its center, spray painted by the Ukrainian American painter Jules Olitski. The picture was not particularly valuable, Goldman had far more expensive paintings, but Kissinger was fond of it.

Before the artwork could be brought into the White House, it was inspected at Andrews Air Force Base to ensure its wooden frame was not bugged. When it was finally hung in Kissinger's office, placed just above the sofa, an elegant man in an expensive three-piece suit was present to inspect the new acquisition. Seeing the canvas with the big purple patch, he turned to Goldman and observed, "Dr. Kissinger is a real intellectual!"

The man, Goldman later learned, was Clemens Conger, chief curator at the White House. As the person in charge of the US government's massive art collection, he was an institution in Washington, and could have supplied Kissinger with any number of world-famous paintings for his office. But Kissinger had his heart set on the Olitski.

Goldman also stood by Kissinger long after he left government. At the age of fifty-eight, Kissinger learned that he would need coronary bypass surgery. Goldman knew that this operation could put people in mind of their mortality. So he told Kissinger's wife, Nancy, that it might be best to tell him they were planning a big sixtieth birthday party. She wholeheartedly agreed. But when Goldman told Kissinger this in the hospital, the response was just a curt, growled "Thank you." Goldman told Nancy Kissinger his idea had been a damp squib. But when he returned to the hospital the following day, Kissinger was sitting up in bed making out a guest list for the party.

In autumn 2019, Kissinger also reminisced about the party, still raving about the "great celebration" his friend Guido had organized at the elegant Hotel Pierre. Colored tablecloths were laid out, rather than the usual white, and the room was filled with brightly colored balloons. The illustrious guests included former US president Gerald Ford and two presidential widows, Lady Bird, the wife of Lyndon Johnson, who had died in 1973, and Jehan Sadat, widow of Egyptian president Anwar as-Sadat, who was assassinated in 1981. Farah Diba, the former Empress of Iran, was also in attendance.

There were no fewer than ten speeches during dinner, including one by ex-chancellor Helmut Schmidt and one by Lane Kirkland, head of the AFL-CIO, the powerful US trade union federation. Marion Gräfin Dönhoff, editor of *Die Zeit*, and Gabriele Henkel, the wife of Konrad Henkel, the long-time head of the Henkel Group, also flew in from Germany to join the celebrations.

Kissinger says his friendship with Goldman was extremely valuable because Goldman never asked for any quid pro quo. Of course, sometimes Kissinger did Goldman a favor, giving a boost here and there to one of Goldman's projects. "But Guido never asked for that, he didn't even expect it from me."

During this period, Kissinger was not the only thing keeping Goldman from Harvard. He also had to take care of his parents and brother in Paris, look after his responsibilities as a trustee and asset manager in New York,

Henry Kissinger's sixtieth birthday dinner, hosted by Guido at the Hotel Pierre in New York City (May 26, 1983). *Right:* Guido with Gabriele Henkel.

attend to his large collection of nineteenth-century Uzbek tapestries, and go to board meetings of the Alvin Ailey American Dance Theater, while also acting as a consultant to Christie's, the auction house.

A lot of Goldman's time was spent on maintaining his ever-growing network of wealthy and influential friends. These now included multibillionaire media mogul Walter Annenberg, an acquaintance of Ronald Reagan, who, through Goldman's mediation, was arranging to donate $25 million to Harvard. Other friends included Barbara Walters—a prominent journalist who brought many useful people to her New York salon—and Brooke Astor, Jane Engelhard, or Jayne Wrightsman, the widows or divorced wives of millionaires, also donors to the Center for European Studies. Goldman, in keeping with social conventions of the time, often accompanied these older ladies to receptions or on short trips as a required male companion.

When the female friends returned to New York from extended vacations or stays at their second and third residences, they frequently found a large bouquet

Left: Guido with Walter Annenberg and *right:* with President Ronald Reagan at Walter's Palm Beach estate, "Sunnylands."

of flowers with a card from Guido Goldman, a master of detail. "My dear Guido," Jane Engelhard wrote in July 1985, "you continue to spoil me with superb bouquets of flowers, one more beautiful than the other, followed by most touching letters, and I don't know how to thank you for this munificence and your continued faithful interest."

Engelhard was the most European of these acquaintances, and the most political. Born in China and raised in France, she had spent the war in Argentina, before moving in 1943 to the United States to marry Charles Engelhard, billionaire owner of a mining and metals conglomerate. One of her four daughters, Annette, later married Óscar de la Renta, a prominent fashion designer. Goldman developed a separate friendship with de la Renta and went to visit his estate in his native Dominican Republic.

Most of Goldman's time and energy, however, went into his most important achievement in the 1970s and 1980s, the establishment of the German Marshall Fund, a new transatlantic think tank.

Jane Engelhard and Guido at her Florida estate "Pamplemousse."

Right: Jayne Wrightsman and Guido at her spectacular New York City home.

Below: Guido, Marietta Tree, and Oscar de la Renta at his Dominican estate.

CHAPTER 7

The German Marshall Fund of the United States

Without question, the German Marshall Fund of the United States (GMF) was Guido Goldman's greatest achievement. Originally founded to investigate and compare social problems on both sides of the Atlantic, its early function was primarily to subsidize European projects undertaken by other institutions, in addition to having a few projects of its own. However, over the last two decades, the GMF has grown into a transatlantic think tank, with a staff of one hundred and fifty-five (in 2001, it had just nineteen). In addition to its headquarters in Washington, DC, the foundation now has offices in seven European capitals, an endowment of one hundred and fifty-seven million dollars (as of December 31, 2019) and an annual budget of $36.4 million (June 2020 to May 2021).

Every year, five percent of the foundation's endowment is spent on current expenses, accounting for around one-fifth of its annual budget. The other eighty percent of the budget comes from external sources. Most comes in the form of grants from governments and from other nonprofit foundations; those funds are used to finance specific GMF projects which, for example, work to promote democracy in eastern and southeastern Europe. Major GMF programs in this area include the Balkan Trust for Democracy, the Black Sea Trust for Regional Cooperation and the Fund for Belarus Democracy.

Despite the name, the German Marshall Fund is not German. It is an entirely American foundation, with interests across Europe, going beyond specific concerns with Germany. The projects it supports cover a wide range of European issues: it is not a specifically German-focused organization. Nonetheless, every year the GMF provides financial support to three primarily German American institutions: the American Institute for Contemporary German Studies (AICGS) in Washington, DC; the American Council on Germany (ACG) in New York, where Goldman served for many years on the board; and the Congressional Study Group on Germany (CSGG), which brings together members of the

US Congress with members of the German Bundestag. In addition, during the 1980s GMF helped to get the Institute for International Economics off the ground, now the Peterson Institute for International Economics.

The three main pillars of GMF are a think tank, a civil society engagement in Eastern Europe, and leadership programs, the crown jewel of which is the Marshall Memorial Fellowship (MMF), a scholarship program for future leaders in politics, business, and civil society.

Founded in 1982 to make young European leaders more familiar with the United States, every year the MMF prepares around seventy people for leadership roles on both sides of the Atlantic. This training is wide-ranging in its scope. Participants receive up to a year of instruction and mentorship in their respective home countries, followed by an intensive travel program to deepen their knowledge about Europe and the US. GMF also organizes meetings between the participants, helping to expand the Fund's extensive leadership network.

Thanks in particular to MMF fellowship alumni, the organization's expanding leadership network now connects some four thousand people in business, politics, media, academia, and civil society. Some MMF alumni have advanced to the highest levels of political and corporate life. They include, to give just a single example, the American politician Stacey Abrams, an African American Democrat who came very close to being elected governor in the state of Georgia in 2018, and, prior to the 2020 presidential election, was repeatedly spoken of as a possible candidate for US vice president. Abrams now plays a key role within the Democratic party. The extraordinary victory of Joe Biden in Georgia in November 2020, turning the state Democratic in a presidential election for the first time since 1992, is also credited in large part to Abrams, who worked tirelessly to mobilize Black voters to register and to vote.

Of course, given the large number of fellowships awarded, there are less laudable alumni, for example the current Hungarian prime minister Viktor Orbán, once a liberal but now transformed into an arrogant, authoritarian right-wing populist. Overall, however, the fellowship program has been a tremendous success, greatly benefiting the work of the German Marshall Fund.

The value and significance of this kind of network can be seen in an example cited by Kevin Cottrell, who was a good friend of Guido Goldman and who has for many years been responsible for promoting young transatlantic talent at GMF. He explains how, since 2002, both American and European soldiers who served in Afghanistan have encountered similar problems on returning to civilian life, including unemployment, social exclusion, and inadequate psychological care. A long-standing Marshall Memorial Fellowship project, run by alumni with seed-funding from GMF, researches their needs.

The purpose of the project is a comparative investigation into the differing conditions soldiers encounter upon their return to the United States and Europe, with a focus on establishing what help soldiers need and the best ways to operate and equip a successful veterans agency. What has to be prevented at all costs is anger and frustration among those returning from war, which can lead veterans to sign on as mercenaries, fueling dangerous conflicts around the world, as happened with veterans of the Serbian army. The risk is considerable and is particularly pressing today, for example with veterans of the conflict in Ukraine.

One MMF alumnus, himself a war veteran, approached GMF seeking support for a project focused on care for veterans. At first, he had a particularly difficult challenge in dealing with the post-2014 situation in Ukraine, where a separatist conflict in the country's eastern regions, the Donetsk and Luhansk oblasts, has been fueled by Russian financial and military support. As a result of the ongoing conflict, Ukraine is now home to around four hundred thousand soldiers who have served in a war zone. But the veterans, once they return to their homes, have been left woefully short of care, abandoned to deal with hardships and trauma alone. Ukraine had no veterans agency and there was no special care for those injured in war. Even President Volodymyr Zelensky, often presented as the great new hope for Ukraine, initially did nothing to establish an assistance program for his soldiers.

However, by providing this small grant to MMF alumni, GMF was able to support setting up a group of experts in the Ukraine to address the issue; and a former fellow advised the panel. Previously a staff member at the US Department of Veterans' Affairs, he was extremely concerned about the Ukrainian government's failure to understand or take action on this problem. He alerted his former colleagues in Washington to the problem, who in turn prompted the US ambassador in Kiev to raise the issue of veterans' care with Zelensky. The Ukrainian president finally accepted the seriousness of the problem, and a new government agency and a program for war returnees were established.

PURE COINCIDENCE

Beyond the size and importance of the organization, there are other reasons why the German Marshall Fund is conspicuous among Goldman's achievements. It is an excellent illustration of Goldman's personal characteristics and his virtues as a human being: prodigious negotiating skills, a never-ending wealth of ideas, chutzpah, persistence sometimes bordering on stubbornness, a talent for establishing extremely durable relationships, and a gift for winning over influential and wealthy people.

Given its emergence during a particularly significant era of West German and American politics, GMF also has historic significance. The genesis and growth of the organization are a story of great ideas and daring, political friendships and rifts, political ingenuity, schemes and vanities. Time and again GMF benefited from seizing the opportunities of the moment.

In truth, the German Marshall Fund largely owes its existence to fortunate coincidence. In fact, before GMF finally was established, the idea almost failed twice, thanks to less fortunate coincidences.

In the fall of 1970—as recorded in a March 1973 memorandum to GMF's first president, Benjamin Read—Goldman was sitting with Stanley Hoffmann at the offices of the German consul in Boston. West European Studies at Harvard, which Goldman had helped to create, was once again running low on cash. The research center, then under Goldman's leadership, was in dire need of funds, needing a million dollars just to keep the lights on. It was not clear where the money might be found.

Goldman had an idea, which he wanted to present to the consul. What would happen, he asked, if you asked the West German government for a million dollars? Goldman already knew how to make the suggestion more palatable to his German audience. June 1972, then two years away, would mark the twenty-fifth anniversary of the Marshall Plan. The Plan had been announced at Harvard in 1947, and the university was keen to celebrate the anniversary. Marshall and his eponymous plan had been responsible for funneling no less than $1.4 billion in postwar reconstruction aid to West Germany. The money was first earmarked as a loan but later reclassified as a gift, with no obligation for repayment. Seventy-five years later, $1.4 billion is the equivalent of almost $14 billion.

So how would it be, Goldman inquired of the consul, if Bonn reciprocated that generous American gesture with a small financial gift to West European

Studies at Harvard? One million dollars would yield about $50,000 a year in interest, enough to keep their heads above water, for the time being at least. West Germany, Goldman went on, must have an interest in ensuring that European studies and academic exchange across the Atlantic continued to flourish at Harvard.

At that moment, for the first time since 1949, Germany was governed by a center left government. An alliance of the Social Democrats and the centrist Free Democrats had beaten the conservative parties in the 1969 federal elections. Willy Brandt—who had had to flee to Norway to escape the Nazis in 1933—now sat in the chancellor's seat.

Brandt had previously served as the mayor of West Berlin. His time running that enclave of the West had taught him well the importance of the United States' support, and the centrality of Germany's alliance with the superpower. This reality gave Goldman hope that his suggestion might fall on fertile ground.

The German consul thought the idea a good one, so Goldman then flew to Washington to try to convince the German ambassador. Rolf Pauls—a career diplomat who had previously been Germany's first ambassador to Israel— was also impressed. He even offered to promote Goldman's idea on his next reporting visit to Bonn, especially to the new foreign minister Walter Scheel.

In fact, Goldman arrived in Germany even sooner than Pauls, having arranged an appointment with the finance minister. Alex Möller, a Social Democrat, was a friend of Nahum Goldmann, and a beneficiary of political favors from him. Möller and Guido Goldman's father had met some years previously through a mutual friend and got on very well. Möller had once been the youngest member of the Prussian state parliament, and had been an early opponent of Hitler, imprisoned for a short time immediately after the Nazi takeover.

Möller invited Goldman to his villa in Bad-Godesberg. As Goldman remembered it, the meeting took place late in 1970, probably in the month of November. There was friendly chat and a good deal of scotch consumed, but before the alcohol could blur his thinking, Goldman made sure to give a short presentation of his idea, telling the finance minister about the difficulties experienced by West European Studies, the importance of academic exchange, and the generous help which had always come from the United States when Germany was in need.

Goldman mentioned the Dawes and Young plans, which helped keep Germany's payment obligations manageable in the wake of World War I. He

Guido visiting Alex Möller in Karlsruhe in mid-1970s.

spoke, of course, about the blessings of the Marshall Plan after the horrors of World War II, reminding his host that the Plan had provided crucial money to get the West German state on its feet. It would be wonderful, Goldman suggested, if Germany could now see fit to help out West European Studies, in honor of George Marshall.

Möller knew all about America's contribution to Germany. Despite not speaking a word of English, he had always been a great friend of the United States. In contrast to some party colleagues, he was an early backer of Adenauer's policy of integration with the West, which had cemented the close ties between West Germany and the United States.

Having heard Goldman's pitch, Möller nodded and got down to business. If Harvard needed two or three million deutsche marks, he said, it could probably be obtained easily enough from Munich Re, the reinsurance giant.

The finance minister had previously served as CEO of Karlsruhe Life Insurance and still had good contacts in the industry.

But then Möller said something else. Pausing for breath, he told Goldman that, as a gesture of thanks for the Marshall Plan, he had a much larger amount in mind. "How much?" Goldman asked, intrigued. "About two hundred and fifty million deutsche marks," Möller replied. Goldman could hardly believe his ears, replying in disbelief: "Minister, I'm afraid your government will never go for that!"

But the finance minister insisted, and pointed out that there was still money remaining from funds once set aside to repay the Marshall Plan. Möller told Goldman to work out a proposal as quickly as possible, which would outline what he called the "intended purpose" of the 250 million marks. A couple more glasses of scotch and the evening came to an end.

* * *

Flying home to the United States, Goldman began to doubt what he had heard. Everyone he had spoken to about Möller's promise said it was a pure pipe dream. Goldman feared he might not even get the smaller sum, the three million marks West European Studies so badly needed.

Several weeks passed without news from Möller: no letter, no telegram, no phone call. Goldman had almost forgotten the conversation with the minister when Möller's office announced that he was to visit Washington in January 1971.

When Möller came to the United States to make his visit, he and Goldman met again, this time in the residence of the German ambassador. Their first two conversations covered various issues, but Möller's big money offer was not raised until Goldman invited the minister to a third meeting, a private dinner at an upscale New York restaurant. Here, Möller suddenly asked: "Well, Mr. Goldman, have you worked out a plan?" He said Brandt had already been told about the proposed gift and had not raised objections.

Goldman had not expected this. In fact, right then there *was* no plan, but there was no way he was about to tell Möller that, and Goldman made sure he did not even suspect it. From his father, Goldman had learned that, at the key moment, some slick bluffing can be essential. Without blinking an eye, he told Möller that he had of course given the matter considerable thought. A large amount of money from Germany should not be wasted, he said. There was also no point in spreading it too thinly: it would be a waste to spend it on founding a dozen professorships at various American universities. What he had in mind, he told the minister, was to establish an American foundation, a kind of bank to which European and American universities and institutions could turn for financial support for transatlantic projects.

When Möller asked what he had in mind more specifically, Goldman told him the proposed organization would promote European issues, academic research, and comparative work on European American questions. Even if the money was German, he emphasized, it should not be channeled toward narrow German concerns.

Then Goldman did the calculations out loud: 250 million marks would be the equivalent of about 65 million dollars. At five percent, that would work out at about $3 million a year. "With that kind of money," said Goldman, "a foundation could do an enormous amount."

Möller was impressed. "Write all that down," he said, "I'll pass the suggestion on to Brandt, and in spring you can come to Bonn and we'll both go to the chancellor and get some business done."

OFF TO THE BLACK FOREST

Four months later, the minister's suggestion had become reality. A meeting with Brandt in Bonn was scheduled for May 13, 1971, a Thursday. The previous weekend, Goldman had flown from New York to London to visit friends, planning to fly on to Cologne that Wednesday and drive the short distance to Bonn in a rental car.

But shortly before he was leaving, he received a phone call in London from Alex Möller's secretary. Completely distraught, she told him that the finance minister had just resigned, angry over his cabinet colleagues' wishes to increase public spending. Brandt had accepted Möller's resignation. Goldman's meeting with the chancellor was off.

Goldman was taken aback, seeing his carefully laid plans crumbling to nothing. Without Möller, the linchpin of the entire plan, there would be no 250 million marks and no foundation. But Goldman had learned another lesson from his father: never lose your nerve in negotiations, never give up when things get difficult, and remember that things can turn in the blink of an eye.

With great presence of mind, Goldman asked Möller's secretary where the former finance minister was, and if he might pay him a visit. "Of course, Mr.

Guido Goldman with Chancellor Willy Brandt and Austrian Finance Minister Hannes Androsch in 1971 in Bonn.

Goldman, a visit from you would be particularly welcome," she said. Möller was in the Black Forest, she told him, staying at the guesthouse of Karlsruhe Life Insurance.

So instead of Cologne, Goldman flew to Zurich, where he was picked up by Möller's driver and taken to the Black Forest, where he checked into a hotel near the guesthouse. The two men met for lunch and dinner, and went walking among the fir trees.

Möller was bitterly, deeply aggrieved, full of anger toward his cabinet colleagues, who had, without hesitation, thrown out his demands for stricter spending policy. Worse, Brandt himself had done nothing, he had simply hung him out to dry, he said. Then the chancellor had added insult to injury by appointing Möller's arch-rival Karl Schiller to his job at the finance ministry, even combining that position with economic affairs to create a new super-ministry. At times, Möller's rage got the better of him, and he shouted: "How can Brandt do this to me? I've known him so long!"

Möller repeatedly emphasized how painful it was for him not to be able to continue with the 250 million deutsche mark Marshall anniversary plan. It had been a really marvelous idea, he said, a cause very close to his own heart. "Unfortunately, I can't help you with it now," he told Goldman, and wished him luck.

But Goldman was not about to give up. There was simply too much at stake, and he still had a number of cards to play. Nearly five decades later, he recounted how he went to a pay phone at the train station—this was, of course, all in the pre–cell phone era—and called Horst Ehmke, Brandt's chief of staff at the Chancellery. Goldman was well acquainted with Ehmke, a former law professor, who had been born in Danzig (now Gdansk in Poland). Goldman had made a note of his private number when he had met Ehmke on a previous occasion. You never know when these things can be useful.

It was a Sunday, and Ehmke was at home. "Listen, I've just spent a few days with Alex Möller down in the Black Forest," Goldman told him. "Really?" asked Ehmke in astonishment and immediately invited Goldman to have dinner with him. "I'd love to," replied Goldman, and explained that he was in any case headed back to Bonn.

When the two men met, Ehmke was visibly upset, shaken—as was the entire government—by Möller's sudden resignation. Ehmke held Möller in great esteem, he told Goldman. But, he added, although the former finance minister was an excellent technical politician, he was too quick to lose his temper. He was no one's idea of team player, always going at things like a bull at a gate, but nobody had imagined he would resign like that. Now Ehmke's SPD colleagues were worried that Möller could resign from the party too, out of sheer pique. "At this of all times," said Ehmke, "as if the government doesn't have enough trouble on its hands."

By the spring of 1971, the social-liberal coalition was not in great shape. Three parliamentarians from the liberal Free Democratic Party (FDP) had broken ranks and crossed over to the Christian Democrats, in protest against Brandt's *Ostpolitik*. The SPD-FDP government was hanging by a thread, its majority alarmingly reduced. Möller was an unusual Social Democrat because of his experience in the private sector, which had earned him the nickname "Comrade CEO." But he had been a pillar of Brandt's government, and was popular both with voters and with the FDP, the Social Democrats' coalition partners.

Ehmke asked Goldman for his advice about the tricky situation. Should Brandt invite his former finance minister to reconciliation talks in Bonn? Would Möller even come if the chancellor asked? "No, probably not," answered Goldman. "So what should we do then?" Ehmke asked him.

At that moment, Goldman had an idea which took a lot of chutzpah. Brandt should go to Möller, he suggested: he should just get in a helicopter and fly over there. "But he can't arrive with nothing to put on the table, he needs to have some kind of attractive offer in the bag," Goldman insisted.

"What kind of offer?" Ehmke asked. "Appoint Möller as the government's official representative for the Marshall Plan anniversary celebrations," said Goldman. "I beg your pardon?" asked Ehmke, in disbelief, "Just repeat that, please." Goldman restated the idea: "Offer Möller an honorary position," said Goldman, "and give him a decent budget. I'm sure he'll go for it. "

Ehmke seemed completely baffled, with no idea what Goldman was talking about. So the American visitor filled him in, telling him all about the dwindling interest in Europe in the United States, and how Möller planned to counteract this with a gift of 250 million marks. "Möller is completely attached to this idea," Goldman told the German. As he told the story later, by the end of the conversation, Ehmke also seemed to be sold on the plan. However, there was no immediate move from the German government. Nothing happened.

Back at Harvard, Guido Goldman sat down to ponder how the request for German funds could benefit West European Studies, as well as getting a possible new foundation off the ground. He talked to Stanley Hoffmann and flew to Washington to ask the advice of Ambassador Pauls and a couple of other close confidants.

After the Möller resignation, Goldman did not know where to turn with his specific suggestions for outlining the "intended purpose" of the German money. He decided to address his proposal to the former minister of finance nonetheless. " It was my feeling," Goldman wrote in his 1973 memorandum, "that I should continue to present my proposals to Möller, despite the fact that he was now out of office." After all, the 250 million marks had been Möller's idea in the first place.

On May 27, 1971, less than two weeks after the Black Forest meeting, Goldman wrote a letter to "the Honorable Alex Möller, former Federal Minister." It began "Dear Dr. Möller," then outlined the proposal for the first funding request, for West European Studies at Harvard.

Harvard has always had strong connections with Europe, writes Goldman in the proposal, attracting many great European minds, especially during and since the grim years of the 1930s. Prominent thinkers of European origin had taught there, including the Austrian economist Joseph Schumpeter, the Russian sociologist Pitirim Sorokin, Paul Tillich, the German theologian and philosopher, and Wassily Leontief and Alexander Gerschenkron, both Russian-born economists. The postwar period saw the arrival of Henry Kissinger to teach political science.

George Marshall, Goldman wrote, had deliberately chosen Harvard in 1947 to announce America's reconstruction program for Europe. As an institution of learning, West European Studies was particularly dedicated to transatlantic relations: there was no comparable institution in the American university system. However, he warned, the survival of the research center was now threatened, because American foundations, including the Ford Foundation, were withdrawing their funding from regional studies.

Two days later, on May 29, 1971, Goldman wrote a second letter to Möller, this time to explain the importance of a new foundation. This letter, too, testified to the deep-seated fear held by figures like Goldman, who had a profoundly transatlantic sensibility, that Europe might fall out of America's field of vision, resulting in long-term marginalization.

Many of Goldman's admonitory sentences still ring true today, having lost none of their force fifty years later. They carry over seamlessly to the Trump era, a time of ubiquitous rampant nationalism, and the growing isolationism in many countries in the face of globalization.

"My dear Dr. Möller," writes Goldman," the generation of prominent American figures who led the drive for European reconstruction is being succeeded by a politically active generation with different concerns." The United States, he said, was increasingly turning its back on the outside world, concerned only with its own problems. To the extent there was interest in other parts of the world, that interest was directed toward the Pacific region.

According to Goldman, common problems should prompt the West to join forces: "Societies on both sides of the Atlantic are confronted by major problems that derive from intense and rapid advanced industrialization."

This is a "fundamental challenge to governments," writes Goldman, best confronted together, through shared and mutual learning. Unfortunately, many Americans still know shockingly little about Europe. "What is needed is a new initiative," demands Goldman, "to make the course of European development more comprehensible in the United States . . . the establishment of an American council for Europe," which would award scholarships, fund research projects, and organize conferences.

The five-page letter also outlined a specific funding proposal for the kind of foundation he had in mind. At least 50 million dollars would be needed, he writes, somewhere between 200 and 250 million marks, paid out in tranches of two million dollars over two and a half decades. He also immediately proposed a name. The foundation, he said, should be named "Marshall Memorial Fund," in honor of George Marshall.

Some days later, on June 6, 1971, Goldman made another trip to visit Möller in the Black Forest. Möller urged him to include Horst Ehmke in his plans: since he was no longer in the cabinet himself, his own influence was now limited. Möller said, he could still get the two or three million marks for West European Studies from the insurance industry, but the 250 million deutsche marks in government money were now no longer his to apportion.

Goldman returned once more to Bonn to put his suggestions to Brandt's chief of staff. Again he urged Ehmke to appoint Möller as the official government representative in all further negotiations. Ehmke agreed, and the following day he presented Goldman's plans to Brandt, who gave his approval.

But for things to be put into practice, Goldman would also have to convince the US government. After all, the planned Marshall Memorial Fund was to be an American institution, based in Washington.

This next step would not be easy. Nixon and Kissinger did not particularly like Brandt, whose social democratic politics were too far left for their comfort. Even if the administration had by and large come to accept the chancellor's new *Ostpolitik* on eastern Europe, reservations remained. The White House feared that the new German policy, which ultimately aimed at détente between western and eastern Europe, might interfere with their own strategic planning toward the Soviet Union.

Brandt flew to Washington in mid-June, where he met with Nixon in the White House. Clearly the chancellor was able to persuade his American counterpart that a German-financed US foundation set up to boost transatlantic relations was a good idea. After speaking with the president on June 15, 1971, Brandt noted: "I spoke to N. [Nixon] about proposals to create a Marshall Memorial Fund to mark the twenty-fifth anniversary of the Marshall

Plan's announcement, linking this to a new American Council for Europe and financial support for European Studies. N. thought this a welcome idea."

Back in Bonn, Brandt finally met Möller, asking him, as Goldman suggested, to organize a large donation for the twenty-fifth anniversary of the Marshall Plan, all on behalf of the German government. Möller agreed, but on one condition: he wanted to negotiate only with Guido Goldman. Brandt agreed.

On July 21, 1971, the chancellor presented the foundation plan to the cabinet, where it was unanimously approved. However, Möller's original proposed sum—250 million deutsche marks—had by now shrunk to 150 million.

The reason for the 100 million cut in funding remains a mystery. Goldman and Karl Kaiser, who as a Social Democrat was well connected to the Brandt government, could only guess. The SPD-FDP coalition, says Kaiser, was very weak that summer, and the Social Democrats probably found it politically easier to get this much smaller sum past their coalition partner, the FDP. But above all, says Kaiser, Möller and Karl Schiller, his successor at the ministry of finance, were sworn enemies. Schiller undoubtedly wanted to get one over on his old rival.

Nonetheless, Goldman was very pleased with the overall result. 150 million marks, payable over fifteen years in installments of ten million, was still an enormous amount, fifty times more than the three million he sought when setting out for Bonn in November 1970.

"THAT DOESN'T WORK AT ALL!"

However, difficulties in implementing the plan were only beginning. The various hurdles that had to be overcome were also a reflection of German American history, fed as it was, and is, by lingering suspicion on both sides.

Goldman wanted a purely American foundation, which would deal primarily with European projects. But others in Bonn had different ideas, especially in the corridors of the foreign ministry. There, it was felt that a foundation paid for with German money should primarily address German American studies. During Goldman's conversations with the ministry, an undersecretary made a further demand: that at least two Germans should have a seat—and a vote— on the foundation's board.

This is exactly what Goldman did not want. He vehemently disagreed, pointing out that a conditional gift is no gift at all. Goldman feared that

German politicians with a say over funding would always be tempted to push for their own interests. He could already imagine the foundation crushed under the wheels of German party rivalries, with politicians of all stripes coming to the president of the Marshall Fund and demanding this favor or that: money for some favorite political issue, a courtesy scholarship for party colleagues or family members, etc.

The mood was tense, with Goldman and the undersecretary each speaking their mind in a frank exchange of views. But Möller put his foot down: "That is out of the question!" he said, coming out in clear support of Goldman, agreeing that the foundation should be a purely American institution. Germans should have no place in its decision-making context. Brandt was of the same opinion.

Möller had anticipated objections at the foreign ministry and had secured Brandt's support in advance. Möller, Goldman said, was like Adenauer in this respect: a strong-willed hard-ass, merciless if he felt he was being messed around with.

Sometime in late 1971 or early 1972—Goldman did not remember exactly when—he went through this experience for himself. At a meeting of the foundation's planning team, the issue of the final name arose. Goldman and the other Americans already knew what they wanted: "The Marshall Fund: A Memorial from Germany."

Möller threw a fit. "No, that doesn't work at all," he grumbled out aloud. If Germany was donating the money, Germany should be the first thing in the name, "Otherwise you can forget the whole thing!" Goldman realizes Möller is absolutely right and gives in: "Let's just call it the 'German Marshall Fund of the United States.'" The name, at least, had been decided on.

IMPERIAL RELATIVES, CIVIL RIGHTS ICONS

Finding suitable members for the board was another complicated process. Goldman wanted at all costs to avoid GMF becoming a cozy Harvard club. He had no mind to face accusations of stacking the board with his own political friends. Although Goldman was registered as an independent, his sympathies were largely with the Democrats. However, he was also well aware that the board of directors must be non-partisan, in other words it must also contain Republicans.

Alex Möller, Guido Goldman, Joe Slater, and Shepard Stone (both of the Aspen Institute) at the founding of the German Marshall Fund (GMF) (June 5, 1972).

Keen to avoid upsetting the Nixon government or the German conservative parties, Goldman wanted as much political balance as possible. He believed that, for its own sake, a foundation like GMF must be able to work with all democratic parties.

In the winter of 1971, Goldman identified the first person he wanted for the provisional board of the foundation, initially known as the "planning group," Robert F. Ellsworth, whom he already knew slightly

Ellsworth, who died in 2011, was a highly influential Republican in Washington, who until the summer of 1971 had served as US ambassador to NATO, after previously representing Kansas in the House of Representatives.

Ellsworth had excellent contacts within both the Republican leadership and the Nixon administration. Moreover, he was a dyed-in-the-wool transatlanticist, a species as good as extinct within the Republican Party fifty years later.

Goldman then asked the Democrat Thomas L. Hughes to join the new board. He did not know Hughes personally but Hughes had been recommended warmly by friends. Hughes was president of the Carnegie Endowment for International Peace, an influential think tank and America's oldest international foundation, which had recently moved from New York to Washington.

In the 1960s, when Goldman had been establishing West European Studies at Harvard, Hughes was already undersecretary at the State department under the Democratic presidents Kennedy and Johnson. Hughes flew with Kennedy on his state visit to West Berlin in June 1963 and was standing very close to him for his famous Ich-bin-ein-Berliner speech in front of Schöneberg Town Hall, which was greeted with loud cheers from tens of thousands of Berliners.

When I spoke to him, Tom Hughes, now ninety-five years old, remembered the astonishment both he and his State Department colleagues felt at Kennedy's sharp tone toward the Soviet Union, which sounded almost militantly hostile to the other superpower.

A few weeks earlier, the president had taken a quite different tone. Speaking at American University in Washington, he passionately pleaded for rapprochement, suggesting that all parties had an interest in preserving the nuclear peace, and calling for talks with the Kremlin to bring this about. Some might castigate this as naïve, or as appeasement, Kennedy told students, but they were utterly wrong. The response from the Moscow newspaper *Izvestia* was enthusiastic: it reported the president's remarks extensively.

"Some of us in Berlin shook our heads back then, at Kennedy's rapid change of mind," Hughes told me in March 2020 at his home in Washington. "But anyone who knew Kennedy as a politician knew how skillfully he adapted his speeches to his audiences. And he did it smoothly and intelligently, he wasn't an idiot like Trump sixty years later," laughed Hughes.

When Hughes joined the German Marshall Fund in the fall of 1971, it was only eight years since Kennedy had been assassinated, and only three years since the murders of both Kennedy's brother Robert, a former attorney general and at the time of his death a Democratic presidential candidate, and Martin Luther King, Jr., the African American pastor and civil rights leader.

It was only seven years since Congress had confirmed African Americans' full and fundamental civil rights, in July 1964. However, the results of centuries of discrimination were still palpable everywhere. In many cities, school buses were set on fire by white parents who did not want their children "bused" to other schools to undermine racial segregation. At the time, no one suspected that half a century later, in summer 2020, the ongoing inequality, humiliation, and stigmatization of Black Americans would once again cause riots in many cities.

1971 was also a year when the Americans and Russians continued their arms build-ups, as well as engaged in a savage proxy war in Vietnam. In both America and Europe, millions of people took to the streets against the war and the latest wild acceleration of the arms race.

Free trade, a key principle of the postwar liberal order, also seemed under threat. Democratic congressman Wilbur Mills shocked the transatlantic community with a draft law offering extensive import protection for American industry. Mills chaired the powerful Ways and Means Committee, which is responsible for handing out federal money, and whose chair is often considered the "secret president" of the United States.

In a style reminiscent of Trump and his America First policies, Mills said in an interview with the German news magazine *Der Spiegel* in 1972: "I want to protect our American industry when imports damage it, when they plunge it into existential crisis, even exterminate it." The German Marshall Fund of the United States was born into hard, troubled, uncertain times.

The advantages of having Tom Hughes on the board were not limited to his political experience, wide-ranging contacts, and profound foreign policy knowledge. He also had a very unusual relationship with Germany.

Hughes's great-great-grandfather had been distantly related to the Hohenzollerns, the Prussian ruling dynasty. In the nineteenth century, he had emigrated to the United States, bringing with him several sea chests filled with old maps, engravings, paintings, writings, porcelain and coins, and he passed on this treasure to his descendants. One hundred years ago, Hughes's father hid the chest in an attic, until the hoard was discovered, much later, by his son. Tom Hughes had always wondered why his father had kept that particular room locked.

The answer was obvious. Hughes's father, a Democrat like his son, had run for political office in Minnesota in the 1930s. Although his family was German

American only to a very small degree, he did not in any way wish this fact to become public knowledge. By then, the Nazis had seized power, and the SS and SA were marching through German cities, fomenting attacks on Jews and boycotts of their businesses. German origins, no matter how distant, did not go down well with many American voters.

Tom Hughes eventually took charge of the sea-chest legacy of his great-great-grandfather, most of which he has since bequeathed to Yale, his alma mater. To the German Marshall Fund he gave six historical maps, now hanging in the large conference room of its Washington headquarters. Only a handful of paintings and engravings now remain on the walls of his home in Washington.

In a way similar to Guido Goldman, Tom Hughes embodies a slice of German American history, history with consequences extending far into the present. Goldman's family fled the Nazis in 1940. In 1938, shortly before the war, because of the family link to the Hohenzollerns, Tom Hughes contacted Wilhelm II, the dethroned German Emperor, still living in exile in the Netherlands, after his hopes of returning to the throne with the help of the Nazis had been disappointed.

Every year, Hughes sent birthday greetings to the ex-emperor, his very distant relative. Every time, Hughes was thanked with an autographed photo. After Wilhelm II's death in June 1941, Hughes corresponded with his widow. Hermine, the dethroned queen of Prussia, left Holland to return to Germany in the middle of the war, moving to Saabor Castle in Lower Silesia.

In 1971, Goldman, Ellsworth, and Hughes became the first directors of the future foundation. Soon they would be joined by others figures, including the renowned physicist Harvey Brooks, and Howard Swearer, president of Carleton College in Northfield, Minnesota. Swearer enjoyed excellent connections to the wealthy Ford Foundation, which had been an initial sponsor of West European Studies at Harvard.

Other board members included the well-known Yale economist Richard Cooper, Carl Kaysen, an economist and expert on international security, and Max Frankel, a *New York Times* journalist, the son of a German Jewish family who had fled from the Nazis. Years later, they were joined by Fritz Stern, the German American historian who had left Breslau in Silesia to go to America with his parents shortly before Kristallnacht in the fall of 1938.

Goldman was also desperately looking for a woman to serve on the board. The German Marshall Fund was, after all, a gift from Germany to the

American people, and he felt strongly that the board should at least partly reflect American society, rather than be yet another association of white men.

Tom Hughes put him in touch with Elizabeth Midgley, whom he respected greatly from their years working together at the State Department. Midgley knew Germany well and spoke excellent German. Alex Möller was particularly enthusiastic about her appointment, Midgley recounted. The former finance minister often felt alienated when English was being spoken by everyone in the room, leaving him unable to understand a word.

Three years after World War II, Elizabeth Midgley moved for a year to Germany with her parents and brother. Her father, a well-known sociologist, was the liaison officer for several German universities in the American zone of occupation.

Midgley and her brother decided to speak only German that year. The family lived in a French barracks in the city of Mainz, which at the time was in the French occupation zone. "We had plenty of heating in the winter," says Midgley, " we were nice and warm, unlike most Germans that year."

Elizabeth Midgley is now well over ninety and lives in an upscale retirement home in Washington. When I visited her, my cup of tea, served in Meissen porcelain, could hardly fit on any surface in the crammed apartment, which was completely full of books, pictures, and souvenirs of all sorts. Germany holds a special place in Midgley's memories.

Her parents had learned German at university; her father had a particular weakness for German sociologists. A photo of him stands on Midgley's bookshelf. He was tall like his daughter, a handsome man wearing the uniform of the OSS, which functioned as the secret service of the US Department of War between 1942 and 1945. At the OSS, Midgley's father worked for the department of research and analysis, and discovered early on the extent and nature of Nazi crimes.

After the war, says Midgley, many Germans had no idea about these terrible crimes, or simply ignored them. They only gradually came to understand what the Holocaust was. "In Mainz, as a young woman with progressive politics," says Midgley, "I was more than ready to tell them clearly, to confront them with the brutal truth."

When she returned to the United States, Midgley eventually graduated from Harvard and was immediately hired by the State Department in Washington. The Bureau of Intelligence and Research, a sort of intelligence service with the State Department, urgently needed Americans with a good knowledge of Germany. Midgley met many German emigrants there, some of whom, like her father, had worked for the OSS during the war.

Even today, Midgley speaks with great enthusiasm about that time, the enormous trove of experience it left her with, the life stories told to her, and the conversations with, as she says, "great minds from Germany and Europe." The Berlin-born philosopher and sociologist Herbert Marcuse hired Midgley, and she was a colleague of the political scientist Franz Neumann, from what is now Katowice in Poland, and of the constitutional scholar Otto Kirchheimer, born in Heilbronn in 1905.

This experience alone made Midgley a great asset to the German Marshall Fund. The foundation's early years, she says, were a very special time. "We were euphoric, filled with an optimistic sense of possibility. We wanted to bolster the new, democratic West Germany." With mild irony, she says that she was not only brought on for her knowledge of Germany, but also because she was, as the only woman on the board, useful for "particularly sensitive tasks": to smooth things over after a dispute, for example, or hint to an out-of-favor foundation president that it might be time to look for another job.

A few years later, Goldman found a second woman to join the board. Moreover, Marian Wright Edelman was an African American and an icon of the civil rights movement, something of great importance to him, as he wanted the board to better represent American society as a whole. Wright Edelman met Goldman in the early 1960s through the civil rights activist Bob Moses, and they remained friends ever since.

Wright Edelman, a Yale graduate, had practiced law in Mississippi for several years, beginning in 1965. She had defended African Americans in court, denounced racial hatred and discrimination, and—via the Head-Start program—campaigned for better education for disadvantaged Black children. Among her closest associates in Mississippi was John Mudd, Goldman's friend from Harvard.

Wright Edelman was an absolutely fearless woman, who did not let a stream of constant death threats deter her from her mission. She worked closely with Martin Luther King, Jr. and Robert Kennedy, both of whom were murdered in 1968, the year she moved from Mississippi to Washington.

Some years later, Wright Edelman founded the Children's Defense Fund, a foundation to protect children and safeguard their rights, to which Goldman made substantial donations. In the early 1970s, the foundation gave a young lawyer her first job: Hillary Rodham Clinton, 2016 Democratic presidential candidate and First Lady of the United States from 1993 to 2001.

As a young law student, Clinton was enthused by a speech Wright Edelman gave about her work at Yale Law School, where Clinton was studying. Years later, writing about her time at the Children's Defense Fund, Hillary Clinton wrote, "Until I heard Marian speak, it wasn't clear to me how to channel my faith and commitment to social justice to try to make a real difference in the world. But she put me on the path of service."

Wright Edelman, now almost eighty-one years old, says she could not refuse Goldman's request to become a board member. "I hardly know a more decent person, or one with a greater sense of justice," she says. As she speaks, she occasionally jumps up to pull out photos from some corner or drawer. Her Washington home is as crammed with memories as Elizabeth Midgley's is.

Marian Wright Edelman brought different life experiences to the very white, very male board of directors, in fact a quite different worldview. As a Black woman, Wright Edelman has developed her own unique way of looking at the 1950s, 1960s, and 1970s, at her own country and at Europe.

After growing up in a small, strictly segregated community in South Carolina, the nineteen-year-old Marian Wright set out for Europe alone. She had just graduated from college, having won a much-coveted Merrill Scholarship for her academic performance, allowing her to travel to Europe for fifteen months.

Wright wanted to get out of the United States for a while, to escape a life marked by injustice. If America had been a place of sanctuary for fellow board members like Goldman, Fritz Stern, or Max Frankel, it had been more like a prison for her, says Wright Edelman. By contrast, Europe, from which so many had had to flee just fifteen or twenty years earlier, felt like liberation to her.

Marian Wright took courses at the Sorbonne and the University of Geneva, went to the World's Fair in Brussels, and toured Ireland, England, West and East Germany, and Poland. She was deeply shaken by the concentration camp at Auschwitz, thinking: "No, South Carolina, my home, with all the brutal injustice of racial segregation, this is still not Auschwitz. Absolutely no comparison. But the racism of many white Americans and the Nazi hatred of Jews come from the same dark, perfidious place in the mind."

Wright also traveled to the Soviet Union. In Moscow she hoped to meet the Black civil rights activist W.E.B. Du Bois, whom she greatly admired. Wright had heard that the sociologist and convinced socialist was to be awarded the Lenin Peace Prize in Moscow. But by the time she arrived, Du Bois had already left for Ghana.

Marian Wright decided to stay on in the USSR for two months. She discovered a love for nineteenth-century Russian literature, especially Tolstoy and Dostoyevsky. She drove to a youth camp in Sochi in southern Russia, where she unexpectedly encountered Nikita Khrushchev, the Soviet head of state, who was receiving the Czechoslovak head of government at his summer residence. Afterwards, she says, so much vodka was served that she, who came from a "family of tea addicts," who had not had even a glass of wine on her trip, got drunk for the first time.

This was not the last time she would encounter Khrushchev. On July 24, 1959, he and Richard Nixon, then US vice president, visited the American National Exhibition in Moscow as part of a cultural exchange program. Wright, then twenty years of age, was just two or three meters away when the two leaders began to spontaneously discuss the advantages and disadvantages of communism and capitalism, with cameras rolling, against a backdrop of an American kitchen. The legendary argument went down in history as the "kitchen debate."

Marian Wright Edelman says that her time in Europe made her a citizen of the world, reason enough for her to gratefully accept Goldman's offer to join the board of the German Marshall Fund. If there were any risk of her worldview narrowing, discussions at the foundation would keep it wide open. "They kept wrenching me out again," says Wright Edelman, "whenever I was about to sink into the little world of my work for US civil rights and child protection."

ON A KNIFE-EDGE

After Alex Möller's unforeseen resignation had almost derailed the entire GMF project in May 1971, it almost fell apart a second time a year later. All had seemed set: Horst Ehmke, Brandt's chief of staff, had just approved Goldman's draft statute and a provisional board had been appointed. But in April 1972, the survival of Brandt's coalition government was suddenly put under threat.

Thanks to the continuing controversy over *Ostpolitik*, the SPD-FDP coalition had lost more members in parliament, leaving their majority wafer thin. The CDU-CSU opposition was planning a vote of no confidence, hoping to attract other dissatisfied members on the government benches, and ultimately to bring down Brandt's administration. The chairman of the CDU-CSU parliamentary group, Rainer Barzel, born in East Prussia in 1924, was bitterly opposed to *Ostpolitik*, and stood ready to take over as the new chancellor. Barzel was convinced he could secure a majority, for which he would need two hundred and forty-nine votes.

Goldman was deeply concerned, fearing that a change of government would bury all hopes of setting up the foundation. Chancellor Barzel would have little interest in saving Brandt and Möller's pet project.

The parliamentary battle of wills was due to take place on April 27. Goldman flew to Germany. On the eve of the no-confidence vote, he sat with Möller in the Maternus restaurant in Bonn-Bad Godesberg. This inconspicuous, old-fashioned wine tavern had not changed in decades, but that was the charm of the place, and it was loved by prominent Bonn politicians.

The Maternus, named after the owner's family, was inseparably linked to the Bonn Republic itself. History had been written there many times over, including German American history. US presidents Truman, Eisenhower, Kennedy, and Nixon had all been guests at Maternus; Adenauer worked out coalition plans with the FDP at the restaurant's tables. If you wanted to know who was hatching plans with whom in Bonn, you went to Maternus in the evening. Until the government's move to Berlin in 1999, the restaurant was widely considered to be Germany's secret control center. It finally shut its doors at the end of 2012.

The restaurant's reputation was why Möller suggested to Goldman they meet at Maternus for dinner on the night before the vote. Goldman was not disappointed. Almost a dozen SPD politicians were gathered at the bar. There were discussions, arguments, gossip. Some of the parliamentarians, Goldman recalls, were red-faced with excitement.

Meanwhile, the FDP was meeting in a back room. Goldman saw the FDP parliamentarian Knut von Kühlmann-Stumm go in, one of the parliamentarians who had already announced he would vote against the government. The FDP leadership wanted to twist his arm one last time, to make clear to him how much was at stake in his rebellion.

The following morning, Goldman sat upstairs in the visitors' gallery of the German parliament. He was nervous: Möller told him that everything will probably be fine, but the conservative parties also seemed confident of victory.

Downstairs in the parliamentary chamber, Brandt came to the lectern to vehemently defend his policies of the last two and a half years. Then the vote was taken. As the ballots were counted, the atmosphere became extremely tense. The announcement of the result was met with dead silence. Rainer Barzel had received 247 votes, two fewer than he needed for a majority. The vote of no confidence had failed, and Brandt would remain chancellor.

The Social Democrats and their coalition partners burst into jubilant celebration, while the conservatives looked on in horror. For Goldman, it felt like a huge weight had been lifted from his shoulders.

However, even with Brandt's victory, Goldman's plans were not yet done and dusted. The federal government had approved 150 million marks for the foundation, payable in ten-million–mark installments over fifteen years. But what about the three million marks for West European Studies that Goldman so urgently needed, with the survival of this institute at stake?

Although Möller had said that he could raise this sum from friends in the Munich reinsurance business, this suggestion now seemed to be off the table. Instead, Möller proposed that three million of the first ten million marks for the German Marshall Fund should be earmarked for Harvard. He told Goldman that Brandt and Ehmke had agreed to this.

This created a problem for Goldman, quite a serious one. How could he explain to the board that, although the new foundation was promised 150 million marks, it would actually only receive 147 million, because Goldman needed three million for his Harvard project? Goldman asked Ehmke for written confirmation that the 150 million marks for the German Marshall Fund come tied to a stipulation from the German government that three million marks from the first installment would be diverted for West European Studies.

Ehmke acceded to the request, giving Goldman a letter which he took to the GMF board. The board was less than pleased, since the German gift had originally been promised as being without strings attached. But, smiling mischievously, Goldman promised them they would soon receive something in return for the money, worth far more than three million marks.

Goldman had another problem, one which he was planning to solve with a clever move. The trouble was that he was wearing two different hats, as both the director of West European Studies, albeit on a brief leave of absence, and as chief negotiator and intermediary for the future German Marshall Fund. He

Board and honorary trustees of the GMF at Adolphus Busch Hall for the founding of the GMF (June 5, 1972).

wanted at all costs to avoid the impression that he was shuffling money from one organization to the other.

Goldman, never slow to pull a trick in business, now turned to Ehmke a second time. In a letter, he told him that the GMF board had expressed major concerns about the terms of the payment. Their doubts could only be alleviated if the German government agreed to the conditions he listed, and confirmed its compliance in writing. Then Goldman outlined, point by point, how Bonn would never be able to ask the foundation for payment or a financial quid pro quo, in any future circumstances.

Horst Ehmke was annoyed by Goldman's chutzpah. He understood Goldman's predicament and sent the letter as requested, but included an explicit note telling him never, ever to ask anything like this again. For the GMF, the signed letter from the chancellor's chief of staff is priceless, to be pulled out in the years to come if a German politician were to ever make an inappropriate demand.

BIG NAMES

On June 5, 1972, the moment had finally arrived. At 11 a.m., in the presence of Chancellor Brandt and Alex Möller, the German Marshall Fund of the United States was launched in a ceremony at Harvard's Sanders Theater.

Goldman's guest list was enormous. The director of West European Studies and interim president of the GMF had invited a who's who of the transatlantic community to Harvard. The legendary John McCloy was there, along with Nelson Rockefeller, the Republican governor of New York, scion of the famous Rockefeller family. Alex Möller was particularly happy about this: as Goldman said, he was fond of having "big names" around.

The staff of West European Studies had typed every invitation on handmade paper. Before they were sent, the then institute librarian recalls, each invitation was carefully examined, literally held up to the light for inspection. "And God help you," laughs Leonie Gordon, "if they found a typo corrected with White-Out. You'd have to write out that invitation all over again. "

June 5 was a bright, beautiful day at Harvard, as it had been, history records, twenty-five years earlier on June 5, 1947, when George Marshall came to the university to announce America's generous gesture to a Europe in ruins. As a gesture of gratitude for the Marshall Plan, Brandt said in his speech, he was bringing the American people a gift from Germany. "By dint of hard work," he continued, "and with American support, Western Europe is now back on its own feet. With the aid of the United States it has again found its own personality. Thus we in Europe, and especially we in the Federal Republic, are deeply indebted to this country."

But this was a day to look to the future as well as the past, Brandt added, warning that "American-European partnership is indispensable if America does not want to neglect its own interests and if our Europe is to forge itself into a productive system instead of again becoming a volcanic terrain of crisis, anxiety and confusion."

Brandt made a promise: so as to secure "peace through cooperation," Europe and Germany would build a shared home with America. "The German

Marshall Memorial Foundation in the United States" would be a contribution to this task. The new foundation would "promote understanding between the partners on both sides of the Atlantic." He was confident, he added, that Europe would "grow into an equal partner" with whom the United States could "share the burden of responsibility for world affairs."

Then the assembled crowd walked the short distance to the Busch-Reisinger Museum, the building to which Goldman's Center for European Studies would move almost two decades later. In the interior courtyard, a festive toast is proposed to the 147 million marks earmarked for the new foundation and the three million for West European Studies. Afterward, at lunch in the great hall, Goldman presented the chancellor with the small Tiffany silver box containing the recording of Marshall's speech. As Goldman's colleague Abby Collins remembers, everyone was in high spirits, outdoing each other with toasts. There was plenty of wine, she says, just enough.

Goldman was pleased that GMF's founding ceremony went off so successfully. Beforehand, of course, his nerves had been on edge. The planning of the ceremony was a tightrope act, almost entirely the responsibility of three people, Goldman and his colleagues Collins and Gordon. None of the three really knew what needed to be done to welcome a visiting chancellor. As Collins says, the experience was one of "learning by doing." Ultimately, however, everything ran like clockwork. As an expression of his gratitude, Goldman gave both staff members the gift of a trip to Europe. Abby Collins flew to Athens at Goldman's expense, while Leonie Gordon chose to go to Paris.

The relationship between GMF and West German politics has never been entirely free of tension, although there has never been an open breach between the two. The Federal Republic of Germany waived any rights to a say over the foundation, but some German politicians have chafed against the rule that the paymaster cannot exert any influence.

The minutes of the board meetings reveal German displeasure at regular intervals. Sometimes a GMF president annoyed the Germans by taking too great an interest in Italy and not enough in Germany. At times, presidents have been regarded as too sympathetic to European social democracy. Some specific GMF programs have also drawn criticism.

In its early years, the new foundation deliberately tried to stay away from major political issues, fearing it would get caught up in party disputes. So the German Marshall Fund turned its attention to apparently more innocuous everyday problems on both sides of the Atlantic. Its first project addressed garbage disposal.

More than anyone, this was the idea of Don Kendall, a GMF board member. The PepsiCo chief executive had recently been appointed by Richard Nixon, a friend of his, to chair the National Waste Disposal Commission, which had just opened a state-of-the-art waste disposal facility in the state of Alabama. West Berlin, surrounded by the Wall, Kendall told the board, does not know what to do with its rubbish. So the GMF invited several Berlin environmental politicians to Alabama.

Not everyone in Germany liked this particular program. Kurt Birrenbach immediately complained to his "dear friend" Guido Goldman. How can it be, he asked, that a foundation bearing the name of George Marshall would first turn its attention to garbage? Birrenbach, a conservative politician, was extremely well-connected in the transatlantic world: president of the German Council on Foreign Relations (DGAP), formerly a foreign policy advisor to Adenauer, and an early supporter of GMF. As chairman of the Thyssen Foundation, he had also previously been the financier of Harvard's German Research Program.

However, exactly the opposite complaint also cropped up, that the GMF was interfering too much in major political issues. By 1975, a substantial number of people within GMF felt the American media was mostly gazing around the world, either failing to report on foreign countries or doing so in the wrong way. In an effort to correct this, it was decided to start the "International Writers' Service," in which well-known journalists—primarily from Germany, France, Italy, Great Britain, and Japan—were asked to write or make radio reports about economic, social, political, and cultural issues in their respective countries. GMF oversaw the production of these reports, had them translated into English, and distributed them to newspapers and radio stations in the United States.

A memorandum from the foundation dated July 10, 1975 states that a number of media outlets across the country had already signaled their interest, including the *Washington Post*, the *New York Times*, the *Nashville Tennessean*, the *Rocky Mountain News* in Denver, and the *Los Angeles Times*.

The project quickly picked up speed. Initially, the pieces published mainly described everyday European matters, including the pollution of groundwater and harsh university admission requirements. Thus in November 1976, Thomas von Randow, science reporter for Germany's *Die Zeit*, wrote "Protecting Privacy in West Germany," an article on the invention of the computer and its implications for citizen privacy and data security.

However, the European journalists hired by GMF increasingly addressed foreign and security policy issues including nuclear armament and the latest disagreements between Bonn and Washington.

The expansion of the themes covered was of concern to some board members. In 1979, Tom Hughes sent a brief note to his colleagues: "Thought we were not involved in international affairs & high politics." *New York Times* journalist Max Frankel even felt the International Writers' Service was competition for his newspaper and stormed off the board.

There were also other reasons for board members to voice criticism. Elizabeth Midgley recalls that, at times, some Republicans were upset about the GMF's perceived closeness to the Democrats. Whenever a Democrat arrived in the White House, the GMF would lose a number of employees to the new government. When a new Democratic administration entered office, the foundation's management floor would suddenly empty out.

Benjamin Read, GMF's first president, went to the State Department to serve in the Carter administration. After leaving GMF, Frank Loy, its third president, became Under Secretary of State for Democracy and Global Affairs at the State Department under Bill Clinton. The current GMF president Karen Donfried has worked under both Republican and Democratic presidents. Under George W. Bush, she was a member of the State Department's political planning group for two years, before returning to GMF in 2005. From 2011 on, she held a number of posts in the administration of Barack Obama, a Democrat, ultimately serving as Obama's Europe adviser.

Former board member Elizabeth Midgley says GMF's closer relations with the Democrats are almost inevitable. Unlike many Republicans, Democrats have always tended to back multilateralism and to see government and the state as an institution for the good of society, not merely a necessary evil.

On the whole, however, criticism of the GMF has always quickly faded away, not least thanks to Goldman's network and his good relationships with all parties, on both sides of the Atlantic.

In May 1974, almost two years after the formation of the German Marshall Fund, Brandt unexpectedly resigned as German chancellor. His fall was prompted by revelations that one of his close advisers had been a long-term spy for East Germany. Goldman was shocked, writing to the former chancellor: "Dear Mr. Chancellor: It was with great sadness that I and my colleagues here at Harvard learned of your resignation. For so many of us in this country you have been a symbol of great leadership in Germany, in Europe, and indeed in world affairs."

On behalf of Harvard, Goldman invited Brandt to come to the university for a few weeks or months, as a way of refueling after the events of the spy affair. "I know," he wrote, "that your time commitments remain very heavy but perhaps you would find some pleasure and interest in being with us for some time. Please consider this a warm and enthusiastic standing invitation."

This letter to Brandt epitomizes many aspects of Goldman's personality, including his loyalty to those who had helped him and his empathy and care for those who have fallen. Moreover, it demonstrates the power of his network

Chancellor Helmut Schmidt at a dinner given in his honor in New York City in 1980 by Henry Kissinger and Guido Goldman with Ambassador Jürgen Ruhfus.

at such moments. Here, his connections with Harvard, West European Studies, and the German Marshall Fund mesh together smoothly, like the cogs of a machine.

Goldman's relations with Brandt's successor, Helmut Schmidt, were at least as good as with Brandt, if not better. Crucially, Schmidt and Goldman's father were friends: they knew and liked each other. When Nahum Goldmann turned eighty-five in 1980, Schmidt traveled to his birthday party in Amsterdam to give a speech.

The second half of the 1970s, however, was a troubled moment in transatlantic relations. The world economy was in crisis, the Soviet Union continued its arms build-up, with the West searching for an adequate response. The Democrat Jimmy Carter had won the 1976 presidential election and taken over in the White House. In the eyes of the arrogance-prone German chancellor, the former Georgia governor was a weak president, not to be taken seriously.

Guido Goldman and Henry Kissinger at dinner for Helmut Schmidt.

Goldman admired Schmidt as a man of action, seeing him as cut from the same real-political cloth as his friend Kissinger. To use the concepts coined by the sociologist Max Weber, Schmidt had an "ethic of responsibility," more than an "ethic of conviction." Schmidt and Kissinger were good friends. Goldman wanted to invite him to Harvard to give the commencement speech at the annual graduation ceremony in 1979, and to award the German chancellor an honorary doctorate.

Schmidt's speech to the graduates came only days before Carter and Leonid Brezhnev met in Vienna for disarmament talks; specifically, they wanted to limit nuclear delivery systems within the framework of the SALT II treaty. In that context, Schmidt wanted to send out a clear message to both. He could hardly get more attention than with a speech on American soil. Although delivered to Harvard students, the actual audience for his commencement speech was made up of the American president and the Soviet head of state.

At Harvard, the chancellor called for the treaty to be signed and ratified quickly, otherwise the arms race could go on forever. As in his sensational speech to the London Institute for Strategic Studies in April 1977, at Harvard Schmidt called on the NATO alliance to better stand up to the Soviet arms build-up. "Our alliance," says Schmidt, "cannot remain idle in the face of this development." It was imperative that NATO modernize its own nuclear weapons.

Few at Harvard that day could have guessed the manner of Schmidt's own ultimate downfall four years later. On October 1, 1982, he was overthrown by a constructive vote of no confidence, with the conservative parties in the German parliament succeeding where they had failed against Brandt.

There were many reasons for the failure of Schmidt's SPD-FDP coalition. But one of them goes back to Schmidt's speeches in London and Harvard. The chancellor's warning was heard loud and clear, with NATO deciding to station nuclear-armed missiles—the famous "cruise missiles"—in western Europe, including Germany.

However, Schmidt's own Social Democratic party was opposed to the measure, with Brandt, now the leader of the party, also withdrawing his support. With the chancellor weakened, the FDP looked to end its arrangement with the Social Democrats and join the Christian Democrats in a new governing coalition. When the vote of confidence was lost, Schmidt was succeeded by Helmut Kohl.

THE "GRACE OF LATE BIRTH"

Goldman was extremely concerned. Unlike Brandt and Schmidt, Kohl knew almost nothing about America. He barely spoke English, and felt less constrained by Germany's dark recent history than either of his predecessors.

Willy Brandt, born in 1913, had fled to Norway after Adolf Hitler came to power. Helmut Schmidt, born in 1918, had been a soldier in the Wehrmacht. Both had been direct witnesses to dictatorship, war, and the persecution of the Jews, albeit from quite different perspectives.

For Brandt and Schmidt, the seriousness of German guilt inevitably meant the country bore a special responsibility, and the integration of West Germany into the liberal western postwar order was a matter of the highest national obligation.

At the time of Germany's unconditional surrender on May 8, 1945, Helmut Kohl was just fifteen years old, as he never tired of reminding audiences when he was chancellor. Many were angered when Kohl proclaimed a policy of "spiritual and moral change." Kohl, a trained historian, described himself as "representing a new Germany," referring to the "grace of late birth" which supposedly spared his generation the guilt of National Socialism.

What *did* the chancellor mean by the phrase? Did he really think his generation could shut the book on the terrible chapter of the Third Reich once and for all, shaking off all responsibility for German crimes? At the time, it was unclear what meaning Kohl actually attributed to the word "grace." Only many years later did he clarify that he had meant nothing more than the coincidence of his date of birth. Ultimately, however, his fear was that the Shoah would be the single determining factor in Germany's image of its history, permanently preventing the country from taking on an independent foreign policy role. In his book of the same name, the historian Jacob S. Eder referred to this phenomenon as "Holocaust Angst."

Relations between Kohl and the German Marshall Fund were strained in the early years of his chancellorship. The German head of government showed little interest in the foundation, thinking it too strongly influenced by German Social Democrats and the Democratic party in the United States. Moreover, Frank Loy, the then president of the German Marshall Fund, was a thorn in the side to some in Kohl's own party. Loy was born in Munich in 1928 and had lived the first few years of his life there, unhappy years for him. Some suggested this was why Loy does not speak well of the country.

Tense relations with the chancellor created new headaches for Goldman. At the end of 1983, he was thinking of the future of the GMF, concerned about possible financial insecurity ahead. Three years later, the German government was due to hand over the final installment of 10 million deutsche marks to the Fund. What would happen after that was anyone's guess. Goldman ideally wanted to ask Bonn for a further injection of funds, another 100 million marks spread over ten years. But how should he go about it?

At the time, Berndt von Staden, German ambassador to the US from 1973 to 1979, who remained on friendly terms with Goldman up to the end of his life, indicated that the prospects for a new cash injection were poor. He told Goldman there would be resistance in the CDU, since it was felt within the party the foundation did not adequately serve Germany's own interests.

In response, Goldman asked his friend Kissinger to have a word with Kohl on his next visit to Germany. The chancellor and the former Secretary of State knew each other, and had considerable mutual respect. However, the chancellor did not want to address the issue, telling Kissinger to speak to Horst Teltschik, one of his close collaborators and confidants. As best as Goldman and Karl Kaiser can recall, Teltschik told Kissinger that the problem lay with GMF's board of trustees. What he meant by this—too many Democrats. This was why Kohl seemed set against providing any further support.

Goldman was grateful for the information Kissinger had obtained: at least he knew where he stood, and where to begin negotiations with the Germans. In early February 1984, he flew to Bonn to meet Volker Rühe, deputy chairman of the CDU-CSU parliamentary group, and its foreign policy spokesman.

Goldman invited him to Petit Poisson, an upscale and outrageously expensive French restaurant in Bonn. Rühe, recalled Goldman, expressed the same reservations as Kohl, but when asked, was unable to say which specific members of the GMF board were a problem. Goldman listed off all the names, quickly getting the impression that Rühe had no idea who they were, let alone which US party they might be affiliated with.

He told Rühe that Marc Leland, one board member, at that time an Assistant Secretary at the Treasury in the Reagan administration, was a Republican, as were General Andrew Goodpaster, a former foreign affairs advisor to the Republican president Dwight Eisenhower, and the lawyer Arlin Adams, a federal appeals judge who was on Reagan's list of candidates for the Supreme Court. Rühe was very surprised, says Goldman.

Later, Goldman dined with Alfred Dregger, chairman of the Christian Democrats in parliament, and the representative of the right-wing "national conservative" wing of the party. Dregger was fond of Goldman and had a more positive opinion of the German Marshall Fund than Kohl.

The most important conversation, however, took place with Kohl's chief of staff, Wolfgang Schäuble. Goldman told him that if the German government, as a donor, was actually so disappointed with the German Marshall Fund, then the best thing would be for the entire board to resign immediately. Schäuble was appalled by the views his party colleagues held of GMF, and promised to work actively for continued backing from Bonn.

Schäuble's support was important, but Goldman knew that if he wanted to permanently secure the future of the German Marshall Fund, he would have to change Kohl's own mind. Ultimately, Goldman would succeed in this, largely thanks to his own social intelligence and the unique power of his network.

Kohl's older son Walter wanted to study at Harvard, while his younger son Peter had his heart set on MIT (Massachusetts Institute of Technology). In the case of Walter Kohl, Goldman pulled a few strings to enable the chancellor's son to go to Cambridge for a time in 1985, where he stayed with the family of the Harvard history professor Richard Hunt.

Goldman and Hunt were friends. At the time, Hunt, the child of a wealthy Pittsburgh industrial family, was the honorary president of the American Council on Germany (ACG). This New York-based association for the promotion of German-American relations had been launched in 1952, along with its sister organization Atlantik Brücke (Atlantic Bridge), at the time based in Hamburg. The major contribution toward setting up the new organization had come from Eric Warburg, the German American banker who found refuge from the Nazis in the United States in 1938. Goldman himself had for many years been an active member of the American Council on Germany. Again, Goldman's connections worked their synergistic magic.

Hunt still remembers Walter Kohl well. In February 2020, six weeks before his death on April 10, the 93-year-old Hunt spoke about their lively conversations around the dinner table and the regular visits from Walter's mother. Hannelore Kohl, he says, showed up in Cambridge every two or three months to see her son. Frequently, on arrival, she would find a bouquet of flowers from Guido Goldman.

"Dear Mr. Goldmann," wrote the chancellor's wife on November 5, 1985, "I would like to thank you very much for your kind welcome to the Hunt house in Cambridge. I was very happy to see my son Walter again during the Boston days at Harvard. He has obviously settled in well, has very good relations with fellow students and professors and seems to be doing great. His first grades are impressive. So, all in all, we can be very satisfied."

Kohl's younger son Peter would soon follow his brother to the Boston area. "During this time, I also went to MIT because of Peter's acceptance," writes Hannelore Kohl. "I think things are going well with that too, especially since Peter scored well on his entrance exam." Hannelore Kohl concludes her letter to Goldman with: "I wish you all the best and also send you warm greetings from my husband."

Maintaining relationships definitely did not hurt. Eventually Kohl gave in, granting the German Marshall Fund a further hundred million marks. However, the foundation had to give five million of this to the Chicago Council on Foreign Relations, an American think tank whose president John E. Reilly was a particular favorite of the chancellor.

Goldman also knew how to use his improved relations with Kohl to benefit West European Studies. In the fall of 1987, Werner Weidenfeld, a professor of politics, was appointed as the German government coordinator for German-American cooperation. Weidenfeld taught in Mainz, capital of Kohl's home state of Rhineland-Palatinate, where Kohl had served as *Ministerpräsident* (state premier) for many years.

In the spring of 1988, Goldman met with Weidenfeld and learned that Kohl, saddened by a lack of interest in Germany among many Americans, was determined to encourage German studies at American universities. The chancellor wanted to set up a number of "Centers of Excellence," Weidenfeld told him, and was prepared to spend a large amount of money, around thirty million dollars. A working group was drawing up an initial list of possible recipients of financial support, he added.

However, the name Harvard was missing from the list. When Kohl found out, says Goldman's former colleague Abby Collins, he was angry: "My son Walter is studying there, Harvard is one of the world's best universities." So Harvard was immediately added to the candidate schools, as were the University of California at Berkeley, Georgetown, Johns Hopkins, Chicago, Princeton, Yale, and a handful of others.

Goldman felt the list was far too long for the available funding. Since he was the only university representative with a direct line to the chancellery in

Bonn, he conducted some tough negotiations with Weidenfeld to pare down the number of possible recipients to three.

The winners were the University of California at Berkeley, Georgetown, the Catholic university in Washington DC, and—surprise, surprise—Goldman's own Center for European Studies at Harvard. The losers, says Abby Collins, were livid. "Who is this Goldman anyway?" some are reported to have said, "He's not even a real professor."

In June 1989, Helmut and Hannelore Kohl came to Harvard for Walter's graduation. Goldman ordered flowers delivered to the chancellor's wife to mark her son's successful completion of his studies. The keynote speaker at the ceremony was Pakistan's prime minister Benazir Bhutto, who herself studied at Harvard in the early 1970s.

That day, all students wore a mourning ribbon in memory of the victims of the Tian'anmen Square massacre in China. Just a few days previously, in a show of bloody force, the Chinese military had crushed the protests of the student democracy movement at the Tiananmen Gate. 1989 would be a fateful year in many ways, both good and bad.

Shortly after Kohl's return to Bonn, his cabinet approved the payment of ten million dollars to each of the three chosen Centers of Excellence, with the money to be paid out the following year. At that moment, nobody suspected that the Berlin Wall would fall only a few months later, on November 9, 1989, making German public money scarce as the country faced the enormous costs of reunification. "Once again, we were very, very lucky," said Goldman.

One year later, on June 7, 1990, Helmut Kohl returned to Harvard. At the behest of Goldman and Richard Hunt, the University was awarding the chancellor an honorary doctorate for his service to Europe and Germany. Kohl would also hold the commencement speech.

However, the recognition for the chancellor did not go unchallenged within the university, and the recognition for Kohl almost failed to materialize. Some members of the selection committee, the so-called Board of Overseers, had little trust in Kohl, now basking in the nickname "the Chancellor of German Unity." They feared that reunification could rekindle Germany's love affair with political strongmen. Kohl's famous phrase about the "grace of late birth" continued to echo down the years, affecting the thinking of many at Harvard.

Others felt that Harvard had already honored too many German politicians. Chancellors Adenauer and Schmidt as well as President Richard von Weizsäcker had all been given honorary doctorates and been invited to speak to the graduating class. Chancellor Ludwig Erhard and Willy Brandt, while he was still mayor of West Berlin, were similarly honored.

But Goldman and Hunt had an important advocate for the plan to honor Kohl: Stanley Hoffmann. When it came to Germany, Hoffmann was perennially suspicious and skeptical, still marked by his painful experiences in Nazi-occupied France during the war. Joe Joffe, editor of *Die Zeit*, recalls how, when he was working at West European Studies in the early 1970s, he looked through the mountains of paper in Hoffmann's office, searching for a dissertation of a German Harvard graduate. Hoffmann asked in astonishment how he came to know this person. He was German, Joffe replied, to which Hoffmann replied that this would be actually a reason *not* to get to know him.

But, since tens of thousands of East German citizens took to the streets to demonstrate for freedom, Hoffmann seemed to have changed his mind on the country. When the wall was opened on November 9 of that year, Abby Collins recalls how Hoffmann, the great skeptic toward Germany, had tears in his eyes and sat in front of television for hours. Hoffmann was ready to lend his support to Kohl.

However, the truly decisive factor was a man named Franklin D. Raines, who had a seat and a vote on the Board of Overseers, the body which decides on the award of honorary doctorates at Harvard. Raines was African American, a graduate of Harvard Law School, and a successful business manager. But most significantly of all, he also served as chairman of the board of directors of the German Marshall Fund.

On November 20, 1989, Goldman sent Raines a "personal and confidential" letter in which he enumerated everything that had been done for Harvard and for German-American relations by Germans, listing off the Krupp, Volkswagen, and Daimler-Benz foundations, private entrepreneurs including Werner Otto and Berthold Beitz, through various German governments.

"Dear Frank," Goldman wrote, ". . . the reason that I am writing to you is to urge you as strongly as I can to support [Kohl's] candidacy." Kohl had consistently promoted American interests, he explained, even if they were extremely unpopular in his own country, including the deployment of American medium-range nuclear missiles. Kohl was a "pragmatic and effective" leader. "I am writing to you," said Goldman, "because I know how much you understand these issues and because I assume you may have a special interest in matters German in view of your membership on our German Marshall Fund board."

At the beginning of December, the Board of Overseers gave the green light to the honor for Kohl. On December 10, 1989, Goldman thanked his colleague from the German Marshall Fund for his commitment to the issue: "I am sure that your involvement was very instrumental in getting the result," he writes to Raines, before describing his most recent experiences in Germany.

Goldman had just returned from Bonn and East Berlin. Rather than "We are *the* people!", the slogan of the early opposition demonstrations in East Germany, demonstrators there were now shouting "We are *one* people!" The path to reunification was clearly mapped out. Goldman was deeply impressed by the peaceful revolution, and by Helmut Kohl. He had just heard the chancellor address the German parliament on the state of the nation and praised his "statesmanlike," prudent policy at this moment of historical upheaval.

Guido Goldman with former President Gerald Ford at dinner for Helmut Schmidt.

Former Chancellor Helmut Schmidt at Nahum Goldmann's eighty-fifth birthday, celebrated in Amsterdam in 1980, at which he was the guest speaker.

"When next we meet, I'll tell you more," he writes to Raines, sharing his confidence that the German Marshall Fund "will respond with useful and interesting initiatives to this new and completely transformed situation in East Central Europe."

A year later, the German Marshall Fund opened an office in East Berlin, just a few hundred meters from the Reichstag. In a letter written on December 20, 1990 to an unknown addressee, Goldman reported enthusiastically about the small opening ceremony. He was completely surprised by how many interesting East Germans had come to attend. "It is manifestly clear that they are yearning for contact with the West—and not just with West Germans—and that the symbolic and real significance of our presence on 'their' side seems to make an important difference to them."

The German Marshall Fund was also gradually launching its first programs to promote democracy in countries of the former Warsaw Pact. But under its ambitious president, Craig Kennedy, the foundation wanted to do much more. Kennedy envisioned turning the transatlantic organization into an international think tank, with interests extending beyond Europe. In December 2012, GMF even opened an office in Tunis, the capital of Tunisia.

The foundation's bold expansion was met with opposition in Germany and it soon came up against financial limits. Every year, the GMF budget came under greater and greater strain, while the assets of the foundation continued to shrink. Goldman, who initially had no objections and sometimes even a liking for the new vision, now feared for the GMF's existence.

Searching for new leadership to refocus on European-American relations, Goldman helped to bring about the appointment of Karen Donfried as head of the foundation in 2014. Forty-two years after its creation, the German Marshall Fund of the United States had a woman as its president for the first time. The former adviser to President Obama on Europe knew GMF well, even having served as executive vice president before moving to the White House. Donfried, who among many other things studied in Munich and speaks fluent German, managed to negotiate further subsidies for the GMF from the federal government. Then foreign minister Frank-Walter Steinmeier acted as an important advocate, supporting funding of two million euros per year for five years, an agreement continued by his successor through 2026.

CHAPTER 8

The American Institute for Contemporary German Studies

Guido Goldman established two major institutions in the 1960s and 1970s—the Center for European Studies and the German Marshall Fund. Nonetheless, a gap remained to be filled. Although both organizations largely relied on German financing, their own institutional focus was not on Germany. This was subject to occasional criticism, including from Chancellor Helmut Kohl. However, the focus of the CES at Harvard and the GMF in Washington was always intended to be on Europe and transatlantic relations, not on a single country, no matter how important or powerful.

In 1983, that gap was filled by the American Institute for Contemporary German Studies (AICGS). For once, the idea did not come from Goldman. It was instead the brainchild of Robert Gerald "Gerry" Livingston, president of the German Marshall Fund from 1977 to 1981.

Goldman was initially skeptical, concerned that the new institution, because of that specifically German focus, might find itself in competition for key donors with the New York-based American Council on Germany. Goldman had close ties to the ACG, since one of its founders was his good friend Eric Warburg, the German American banker.

Livingston was able to dispel Goldman's concerns at a meeting in February 1982. After speaking to Livingston, Goldman was hugely enthusiastic about the proposal, offering the former GMF president advice and working to secure financial backing from the GMF for the new venture. The proposed AIGCS could also serve to appease those in Bonn who still felt the GMF did not give enough attention to Germany.

Livingston was a Harvard alumnus like Goldman, but he had attended the university ten years prior to Goldman. After graduation, he entered the US diplomatic service in 1956, going on to multiple postings in Germany, including West Berlin, the Hamburg consulate, and the embassy in Bonn. He also served in Salzburg and Belgrade.

In 1974 Benjamin Read, the GMF's first president, hired Livingston to be his second-in-command. Read was sometimes accused of an ambivalent relation to Germany, and of being better informed about Italy than the country financing his organization. For this reason, he wanted a proven German expert at his side. Three years later, when Read moved over to the State Department, Livingston stepped into his shoes as GMF president.

For some on the GMF board and in the Bonn political establishment, Livingston seemed considerably too close to European social democracy and took too much of an interest in day-to-day politics. Back in the late 1960s, he had been fascinated by the new thinking about Bonn's relations with East Germany and the other eastern European states, exploring these ideas in a working group at the Council on Foreign Relations, a leading New York think tank. In 1981, Livingston was replaced as GMF president, moving to Georgetown University, where he began to work on a book on German foreign policy.

There was no shortage of material for his writing. The thaw in relations brought about by Brandt's *Ostpolitik* had come to temporary halt, and tensions were rising between East and West. The Soviet Union was determined to station medium-range missiles in eastern Europe, including its East German client state (GDR). The Western defense community responded to the provocation in the form of NATO's famous decision on a "two-track" strategy. This entailed simultaneously offering the Kremlin disarmament talks, while also warning that it would station its own medium-range missiles in western Europe, including in West Germany.

The situation came to a head with Moscow's invasion of Afghanistan at the end of 1979. The Kremlin desperately wanted to prop up their wobbly communist puppet regime in Kabul. Meanwhile, in Poland, an increasingly dissatisfied population was rising in protest against their government. Strikes broke out, and the independent trade union Solidarność was founded in the summer of 1980, soon attracting almost ten million members. In the West, there was considerable anxiety that—as in Hungary in 1956 and Czechoslovakia in 1968—Soviet troops might invade to secure Kremlin rule.

On December 11, 1981, Chancellor Helmut Schmidt undertook a three-day visit to East Germany, looking to send a cautious message of détente at a particularly turbulent moment. But while Schmidt was in East Germany, the Polish government, with the knowledge and support of the East Berlin regime, imposed martial law. The tens of thousands of Polish soldiers mobilized against Solidarność cast a dark shadow over the meeting between Schmidt and Erich Honecker, chairman of the GDR's State Council.

The GDR was up to its neck in financial troubles, with foreign debts amounting the equivalent, in today's terms, of twenty-two billion euros. Its currency was spiraling downward on the financial markets. In urgent need of assistance, East Berlin asked the West for cheap loans, and sought Bonn's support for its application to join the International Monetary Fund.

Years later, writing in *Die Zeit*, Helmut Schmidt recalled that conversation with Honecker: "He believed in all seriousness that the GDR had created a 'world class' economy and was one of the most important industrial nations in the world. But at the same time, he worried about the weak exchange rate of the East German mark and about the country's foreign exchange crisis."

On the other side of the Iron Curtain, the Bonn Republic was also seeing troubled times. Its economic performance was weakening, and NATO's two-track strategy had met with resistance across large swathes of the population. Eventually, the coalition government between the Social Democrats and the Free Democrats ran into trouble, and on October 1, 1982 Schmidt was toppled in a vote of no confidence, to be succeeded as chancellor by Helmut Kohl.

Gerry Livingston was increasingly concerned. Developments in the Federal Republic had a direct impact on German-American relations, but there was no institution in which they were subjected to scholarly investigation. Of course, German issues were never completely ignored, they were too important for that. The situation was discussed in the CES and the GMF, as well as in other institutes and think tanks. But no permanent institution existed which could be a center for sustained investigation with the necessary academic rigor.

The problem, above all, was Americans' ignorance of East Germany. What happened and what was thought east of the Oder-Neisse line was, at best, a topic for seminars on the USSR and the rest of communist eastern Europe. There was zero contact with politicians and scholars in East Berlin, Rostock, or Leipzig.

Livingston wanted to change all that. He took his idea to the dean of Georgetown University, as well as to Steven Muller, then president of the Johns Hopkins University. Muller, also a GMF director, was immediately enthusiastic, for reasons similar to those that had led Goldman to found the CES and the GMF.

Muller had been born Stefan Müller in Hamburg in 1927. His father, a Jewish lawyer, was sent to Sachsenhausen concentration camp after Kristallnacht, but was miraculously released soon after. He immediately fled with his family, first to England, then to the United States. Like Goldman, ten years his junior, Muller was committed in the postwar period to maintaining good German-American relations. He was awarded West Germany's Federal Merit Cross in 1980.

Muller was also firmly convinced that a German institute would be a good match for his own university and thought this should be clear in its name. Hence the institute's full title: American Institute for Contemporary German Studies at Johns Hopkins University.

Founded in 1876 with a bequest from Johns Hopkins, Johns Hopkins University was guided by the ideals of Wilhelm von Humboldt, who thought scholarship and research should go hand in hand. (New research has recently revealed that Hopkins was the owner of several enslaved people before the Civil War. In the aftermath of the conflict, he became a determined opponent of slavery.) Today, Johns Hopkins is one of the best teaching and research institutions in the world, renowned above all for its schools of medicine and health care in Baltimore, and for the School of Advanced International Studies (SAIS) in Washington.

To launch the new institute, the Johns Hopkins president offered an interest-free loan of three hundred and fifty thousand dollars and also convinced several donors in Germany and America to support the AICGS. As with the Center for European Studies, the AICGS depends on private donations to survive, hence the presence of many businesspeople on its founding board and later on its board of trustees.

Muller and Livingston's favorite candidate to be director of the new institution was George Shultz, the Republican politician and businessman. But in summer 1982, Shultz became Secretary of State in the Reagan administration. Next on the list was Donald Rumsfeld. Everyone, including Goldman, thought this was a good idea. So did Rumsfeld.

At the time, Rumsfeld enjoyed an impeccable reputation in both Germany and the United States. He had an excellent network in both politics and business, and there were no doubts within the AIGCS about their choice. It would be two decades later—a time when Rumsfeld had nothing to do with the AICGS—that he became a highly controversial figure who attracted violent hostility.

Rumsfeld was of German ancestry. In 1969, the same year as Kissinger, he joined the Nixon administration, and in 1975 became the youngest ever US defense secretary, under President Ford. Between 2001 and 2006 he held the defense portfolio a second time, this time in the administration of George W. Bush.

After the terrorist attacks of September 11, 2001, Rumsfeld organized the invasion of Afghanistan and strongly advocated for an attack on Iraq. A hardliner, he eventually fell from grace and was forced to resign in 2006. His strategy in the Iraq war, in which hundreds of thousands were killed, was a failure. In addition, as a US Senate investigation later established, Rumsfeld was responsible for the military's "aggressive interrogation techniques" in the campaigns he oversaw. These torture methods included sleep deprivation, sexual humiliation, and intimidating prisoners with dogs. Above all, however, his name is associated with the notorious technique known as "waterboarding," or "simulated drowning," in which a victim is bound, their nose and mouth covered with a cloth, and then has water poured over their head until they think they are about to suffocate to death. Because of this practice, an alliance of lawyers and human rights activists in Germany reported the former defense secretary to German federal prosecutors, seeking a prosecution for war crimes.

In 1983 this could have been predicted by no one, of course. At that time, Rumsfeld was head of the pharmaceutical company G. D. Searle, and widely respected across party lines on Capitol Hill. He recruited numerous influential figures to serve on the founding board of the AICGS, including Guido Goldman. On February 18, 1983, Goldman wrote to Rumsfeld: "Dear Don, I am delighted to join the Founding Board of the new Institute and particularly look forward to working with you on this important enterprise."

Rumsfeld did considerable service at the AICGS. The institute would become a place where American politicians, business leaders, journalists, students, and scientists could deepen their knowledge of Germany. One enormously important aspect of its work, largely a secret at the time, took place in the 1980s, when the AICGS allowed Germans from both sides of the Iron Curtain an opportunity to meet, providing a space of encounter for politicians and academics from East and West.

Neither Muller nor Livingston could have foreseen the opening of the Berlin Wall on November 9, 1989, followed by the swift collapse of Soviet rule in Eastern Europe. But both had a keen sense that a subterranean change was afoot, especially in relations between East and West Germany, states that were repeatedly caught in the crossfire of the Cold War.

In November 1983, Livingston traveled to East Berlin to meet Claus Montag, head of the foreign affairs department of the GDR Institute for International Relations. "Dear Professor Montag," he wrote to him, in perfect German, a few weeks after the encounter, "I would like to thank you again very much for your hospitality and the rewarding discussions in Berlin at the end of November. As Steven Muller and I continue to try to establish the new institute, I hope to deepen and increase my knowledge of and acquaintances and friendships in the GDR."

At this point in its existence, the GDR had, so to speak, its back to the wall. Insolvency threatened, and the East Berlin government was increasingly reliant on the support of Bonn. Ironically, it was Franz Josef Strauss, state premier of Bavaria, chairman of the conservative Christian Social Union party, and famous as a hardline anti-communist, who met with Erich Honecker to arrange a billion-euro loan, saving East Germany from state bankruptcy.

There were other signs of a gradual easing of tensions. In February 1984, intellectuals from both West Germany's Social Democrats and East Germany's ruling Socialist Unity Party (SED) met for the first time, in the town of Wendisch Rietz in the state of Brandenburg. On the agenda was the future of work, the shaping of society, and ecological questions. More generally, participants sought to sound out possible areas of agreement and identify topics where irreconcilable differences remained.

The participants were nervous. Especially for the Social Democrats, the meeting was heavy with historical resonance. The fateful handshake between the Communist Party's Wilhelm Pieck and the Social Democrat Otto Grotewohl in April 1946 was painfully engraved on their memory.

That handshake symbolized, more than any other moment, the disappearance of the Social Democratic Party in the Soviet-occupied zone, as Grotewohl and Pieck agreed to merge the SPD and Communist Party to form the SED. The Communists took command, and Social Democrats in East Germany were doomed to forty years in the wilderness.

But by the time of the Brandenburg meeting, that disgrace lay almost four decades in the past. Willy Brandt, now serving as SPD chairman, had no objections to the dialogue, especially since, as history showed, the communists now had much more to fear than the SPD. In the rivalry between systems, the liberal, democratic Federal Republic had proved far superior to the socialist dictatorship in the East. People fled in one direction only, from East to West.

In August 1987 the two parties published the results of their dialogue, to divided reaction in West Germany. Many were outraged by the joint discussions, including a lot of SPD members. As soon as the dialogue became public knowledge, many within the party protested at what they regarded as premature rapprochement, indeed a kind of ingratiation with the regime in East Berlin, which was responsible for widespread human rights violations against its own citizens. In 1983, a substantial group of Social Democratic university lecturers had published an appeal in angry opposition to their party's new policy. These included Goldman's friend Karl Kaiser, as well as the historian and former Kennedy scholarship holder Heinrich-August Winkler, and Gesine Schwan, a member of the SPD's Commission on Basic Values. For some time, this group had felt alienated by the SPD's direction; above all, they were infuriated by the stalling tactics used against NATO's twin-track strategy by many in the party. They thought the party had become too naive about communism and the Soviets. Ex-Chancellor Helmut Schmidt was another opponent of the SPD-SED dialogue. In his book, *Companions: Memories and Reflections*, he referred to the talks' final declaration as a "morally and politically absurd" pamphlet.

But in East Germany, the party newspaper *Neues Deutschland* sold like hotcakes, literally torn from the hands of street vendors. Holding the joint SPD-SED declaration in hand, church representatives and civil rights activists demanded freedom of expression. The document, after all, stated that both parties had committed to "open discussion about competition between the two systems, their successes and failures, advantages and disadvantages." Twenty years later, the German news magazine *Der Spiegel* would write: "The bottle had been opened and the genie slipped out; East Germany's rulers could no longer keep hold of the opposition ghost."

As influential as the dialogue was in retrospect, its importance can be overestimated. The key reason behind the growing desire for freedom and the increasing daring of the East German opposition was not in Bonn or East Berlin, and neither in the SPD nor the SED. The key figure sat in Moscow, at the heart of the Kremlin: Mikhail Gorbachev, head of the Communist Party of the Soviet Union. Since March 1985, it had been Gorbachev who had determined the fate of his country, as his policies of *glasnost* (openness) and *perestroika* (reconstruction) gradually opened the door to the end of the Cold War, including Soviet rule over Eastern Europe.

Gerry Livingston's American Institute for Contemporary German Studies also wanted to encourage the growing readiness to talk among both East and West Germans. The AICGS organized conferences, seminars, and round tables, especially on economic development. Livingston's contacts in East Germany were primarily in the Institute for International Relations and the Academy of Sciences in East Berlin. Participants in these events included figures like Hans-Jürgen Misselwitz, the biochemist and civil rights activist, but also hard-headed members of the regime, including Hermann Axen, a member of the GDR's ruling politburo.

In November 1987 Gerry Livingston wrote to Steven Muller: "We should know with whom we are dealing. Axen is no reformist Gorbachev. He is an old-time, hardline former Stalinist . . . I have no problem inviting him, but others on our Board know or will be told about him and his background, no doubt."

Hanns-Dieter Jacobsen, professor for economics at the Free University in West Berlin, attended these events time and again, a frequent and welcome visitor to the United States. In 1978 he received a Kennedy scholarship to the Center for European Studies at Harvard, where he befriended Goldman's colleague Abby Collins. In 1984 he came to Washington on a fellowship, working at both the AICGS and the Center for Strategic and International Studies at Georgetown. He also, among other things, lectured at Stanford University in California and gave lectures at the German Marshall Fund.

Jacobsen was a highly respected scholar, whose main topic of interest was trade relations between East and West Germany. In 1992 he was exposed as an East German spy and given a suspended sentence for espionage.

It turned out that Jacobsen had been working as an "Inoffizieller Mitarbeiter," a so-called unofficial collaborator for the East German regime since his student years. The shock was huge, says Abby Collins, who unsuspectingly visited Jacobsen in Berlin in the early 1990s and allowed him to guide her through East Berlin and Potsdam.

An internal AICGS document stated that: "Jacobsen allegedly reported to 'Section XI—the USA and its organizations in Europe' of the intelligence division of the MFS [the Ministry of State Security, better known as the Stasi]. He supposedly delivered the material in the form of film hidden in specially prepared spray cans." However, in all this time, there was nothing secret to report from the AICGS, the CES, or the Marshall Fund, whose events were always entirely public. The Jacobsen affair caused some horror but ultimately no harm.

In 1989, Livingston brought Jackson Janes, an expert on German-American relations, to the AICGS. The two men had known each other since they worked together at GMF. When Livingston was president at that organization, he had hired Janes as head of its European office in Bonn. Janes had already spent several years in Germany as director of the German American Institute in Tübingen and as an instructor of American Studies at the University in Gießen.

Prior to and after the fall of the Berlin Wall, Livingston urgently needed help. Inquiries were flooding in to the AICGS from American journalists, politicians, and companies, all of whom suddenly wanted to know what was going on in Germany and in Europe. They needed Americans who could explain it all to Americans: Jackson Janes was very well equipped for that.

It goes almost without saying that Goldman also had a hand in this hire. Although on a several-year hiatus from his formal service on the of the AICGS, Goldman retained a say in hiring for important positions. Like Livingston, he has been familiar with the energetic Janes since his GMF years in Bonn. Goldman had often visited him there and remained very fond of him.

In 1994, Livingston resigned, and Janes was chosen to succeed him as executive director, together with his colleague Lily Gardner Feldman, the Institute's renowned director of research. When Feldman returned to academic life at Georgetown University in 1996, Janes remained AICGS's executive director, later renamed president. Livingston stayed affiliated with the Institute for a couple of years and helped to strengthen its financial platform.

It was, in general, an era of upheaval and new directions, and Germany faced ever-increasing challenges and demands. It was no longer a question of figuring out how to rejoin two separated parts. Instead, the issue was a united Germany's increasingly important role in Europe and the world, and what the country would do with it.

Janes would eventually retire in 2018, to be succeeded by the political scientist and diplomat Jeff Rathke. Both Guido Goldman and Karl Kaiser warmly recommended him to the AICGS's board of trustees. The two had dinner with Rathke, and at the end of their conversation they were deeply impressed by his knowledge of Germany, his dynamism, and his experience in the world of diplomacy and think tanks.

However, Rathke had already scored points in Goldman's eyes even before he and Kaiser cross-examined him on his intentions, his plans, or the role of

Germany in the Trump era, a moment when the country was widely hailed as the new beacon of hope for the liberal international postwar order.

Rathke, as he remembers with a smile, first had to listen to Goldman speaking about this and that, including how he had donated his extensive collection of *ikats* to various US museums. Pronouncing the word *ikat*, Goldman paused a moment, assuming no one, including Rathke, would know what it referred to: a particular weaving technique for tapestries and fabrics for clothing, used in certain parts of Asia. But before Goldman could explain, Rathke confirmed he already knew what they were. "My wife," he laughed, "has been collecting southeast Asian *ikats* for years." Rathke, one; Goldman, zero.

CHAPTER 9

Shadows of the Past

THE JOHN MCCLOY CONTROVERSY

Goldman was involved in two other projects when the American Institute of Contemporary German Studies was being established in the early 1980s. The first of these was the American Council on Germany (ACG), a German American association based in New York. Since its founding in the early 1950s, the ACG had been particularly concerned with good transatlantic economic relations. The ACG urgently required money to hire a much-needed full-time director. Goldman persuaded the Krupp Foundation to donate two million deutsche marks, money the ACG used to set up the John McCloy Fund.

Shortly before this, the Volkswagen Foundation announced it would donate two million marks to Harvard University to set up a scholarship program for talented German students to spend two years at the renowned Kennedy School of Government, a program to be called the John McCloy Fellowship.

Everyone was happy with these new plans, because German-American relations had once again hit a rocky patch. With hawkish Ronald Reagan, there was again a Republican in the White House. Chancellor Helmut Schmidt made no secret that he thought little of this California actor. In addition, NATO's twin-track strategy on missile deployment repeatedly caused tension between Bonn and Washington.

For this reason, the Volkswagen Foundation wanted to make a generous gesture to mark its own anniversary, demonstrating to Americans that the United States was regarded in Germany as a good friend and irreplaceable ally, all disagreements notwithstanding. At this point, no one remotely considered that the McCloy name might come with a bitter aftertaste for some, or that a John McCloy Fellowship at Harvard might meet with opposition.

For the American Council on Germany the name was an easy choice. McCloy enjoyed an excellent reputation in transatlantic leadership circles: along with the banker Eric Warburg, he founded the ACG in 1952. In the postwar years, as the US high commissioner, he made outstanding contributions to the reconstruction of West Germany.

Without McCloy, Germany would probably have taken longer to get back on its feet. The US high commissioner listened to Warburg's advice, who warned against dismantling German industry. Even as assistant secretary of state in the Department of War in 1944, McCloy opposed then Treasury Secretary Henry Morgenthau's plan for extensive deindustrialization of postwar Germany. The steel conglomerate Krupp, among many others, were beneficiaries of McCloy's policy.

The name McCloy was also a foregone conclusion for the Volkswagen Foundation. The idea for its new program did not come from the carmaker, however. It went back fifteen years, to Shepard Stone, another important figure in postwar transatlantic relations, especially German-American relations.

The story of Shepard Stone must be told briefly to make the context of the time understandable and to illustrate again how the various threads always seem to come together in the figure of Guido Goldman.

Stone, born in 1908 in New Hampshire, the son of Jewish emigrants from Lithuania, studied politics and history at Heidelberg and mainly in Berlin before the war. A few months after Hitler came to power, he married Charlotte Hasenclever-Jaffe, returned with her to the United States, and became a journalist for the *New York Times*. Stone fought as a volunteer with the US Army in Normandy in 1944 and rose to the rank of a major. He visited the Nordhausen and Buchenwald concentration camps after they had been liberated.

But, while being horrified by what he saw, it did not change his basic positive attitudes toward Germany. In fact he soon clashed with his American superiors who took a punitive approach toward the defeated country. Strongly disagreeing with them, Stone went back to the US and to the *New York Times*, writing reports on developments in West Germany. Like the Goldmanns, Shepard Stone advocated for the country's reintegration into the Western community of democratic nations.

He returned to West Germany and helped to build a free press and culture system in various locations within the American sector always in close contact with the US High Commissioner John McCloy. In 1950 Stone was appointed to McCloy's inner circle, where he took charge of public relations.

When McCloy returned to New York and became a trustee of the Ford Foundation, he took Stone with him to develop their European program.

This included support for the Congress for Cultural Freedom (CCF), an anti-communist cultural organization founded in 1950 in Paris, which sought to influence the discourse of left-wing European intellectuals and was covertly funded by the CIA. Numerous liberal and left-wing commentators were associated with the Congress for Cultural Freedom in the years after the war. Stone was an early backer of the organization. It turned out later, however, that some members of the Congress were US spies and that it received much of its money from the CIA, funneled indirectly through the Ford Foundation.

In 1966/67, the CIA support became public knowledge, causing an enormous scandal. McCloy had left the Ford Foundation and its new president asked Stone to step down. The CCF was reorganized as the International Association for Cultural Freedom (IACF) and Stone, now jobless, was hired to run it from Paris. He tried to get foundation funding but was not very successful. At that point Willy Brandt heard of Stone, sitting in the French capital and unhappy, and hatched a plan: the German chancellor did not find in Washington the support for his *Ostpolitik* he was hoping for. Brandt, therefore, felt that bringing a pro-German American like Stone to Berlin as the director of the Berlin Aspen Institute would help German-American relations.

In 1974, Shepard Stone returned to his beloved West Berlin, where he ran the Aspen Institute for fourteen years, at the time the most prominent site of German-American dialogue. In the 1970s and 1980s, Aspen hosted just about everyone committed to strengthening the international liberal postwar order: Willy Brandt and Richard von Weizsäcker, later mayor of Berlin and president of Germany, respectively; Helmut Schmidt and Marion Gräfin Dönhoff, editor of *Die Zeit*; the publisher Axel Springer and the CDU politician Kurt Biedenkopf; Henry Kissinger and John McCloy; and of course Karl Kaiser and Guido Goldman, many times.

Jim Cooney was Stone's deputy at Aspen between 1978 and 1982. Inevitably, it was Kaiser and Goldman who recommended him for the position. At Harvard, Cooney had studied politics with Kissinger and Hoffmann in the sixties. Kaiser awakened his enthusiasm for Germany in his seminars, and also introduced him to Goldman. In early 1983, Goldman brought Cooney back to Harvard. Cooney had mastered the art of networking and cultivating relationships at the Aspen, and he was now to co-lead the McCloy Fellowship with Goldman. In practice this meant he ran it, since Goldman had half a dozen other commitments and was rarely seen at Harvard. Cooney's assignment was to get the new program up and running and if possible, lead it into the future.

Cooney knew the origins of the McCloy Fellowship better than anyone. While still working at the Aspen Institute, Stone showed him a paper he had written in the mid-1960s: a memorandum for a graduate student fellowship in honor of John McCloy.

What Stone had in mind was an equivalent of the Rhodes Fellowship. In the United States, the Rhodes Scholars form one of the most exclusive clubs. Thanks to money donated by the British imperial tycoon Cecil Rhodes, every year a small group of students—largely American, although before World War II there were some Germans among them—have been able to spend two years of graduate study at Oxford University. Some Rhodes alumni have gone on to great success, including Bill Clinton, forty-second president of the United States. Something like the Rhodes scheme, says Cooney, was unquestionably what Stone had in mind for German students.

Stone—along with Goldman and Kaiser—was delighted when Volkswagen picked up on the idea in the early 1980s and offered to provide finance. After returning to Germany from Harvard in 1968, Kaiser acted as adviser to the Volkswagen Foundation. There was some initial uncertainty about what institution would be home to the new project, but, along with Goldman, Kaiser ensured that the McCloy Fellowship ended up at Harvard, where it found a permanent home at the Kennedy School of Government. Here, German graduates were to be trained for two years, in preparation for demanding public roles in Germany and at international organizations.

However, protests—restrained at first, then more and more vociferous— arose in response to the program's official launch in 1983. Critics and defenders of the name fought a bitter running battle for months, in the long shadow of McCloy's past work for the Department of War and as high commissioner to West Germany.

McCloy was accused of three problematic actions, all of which were basically undisputed by both sides. First, as assistant secretary of state at the War Department, McCloy was jointly responsible for the internment of around 120,000 Japanese American civilians after the Japanese attack on Pearl Harbor in December 1941. The internees, mostly from the US west coast, were collectively classified as a national security threat, forcibly relocated, and imprisoned in hastily built camps, far inland.

The order to intern these people was signed into law by President Franklin Roosevelt. Executive Order 9066 declared large parts of California, Oregon, and Washington to be restricted areas. A key figure responsible for the execution of EO9066 was Earl Warren, the Republican attorney general of California, later renowned as an arch-liberal Chief Justice of the United States.

Second: as a senior War Department official, shortly before the end of the war, McCloy advised the president against bombing gas chambers and crematoria at Auschwitz, along with the railways leading to the extermination camp.

Third: in 1951, as high commissioner to West Germany, he pardoned Alfried Krupp, a war criminal sentenced to a long prison term at the Nuremberg trials. Worse, McCloy returned confiscated property to the Krupp conglomerate, which had grown even wealthier with manufacturing during the war, including the use of labor of enslaved people.

Leading the rebellion against McCloy in the spring of 1983 was the Harvard law professor Alan Dershowitz; among America's best-known criminal defense lawyers, he was a sharp-tongued prosecutor and a political hothead. He was also of Jewish heritage. "Rarely," he wrote about McCloy in the Boston Herald, "in the annals of American history has one man participated in so much evil." Jewish and Asian student groups joined the protests, and *Washington Post* commentator Richard Cohen, enraged, wrote that the choice of name was "merely a disgrace," but no surprise, since Harvard is "is to the Establishment what China is to pandas."

McCloy defended himself, writing in the *New York Times* that, "We all share the conclusion that the evacuation was traumatic for the 120,000 resettled." But he said that, even in retrospect, the internment of Japanese American civilians was justified. He expressed no reservations. Unlike Earl Warren, who was in fact far more complicit than McCloy, he acknowledged no need to apologize to victims, and was opposed to any compensation payments. Five years after the Harvard controversy, in 1988, Congress authorized further payments to those rounded up during the war.

As defenses go, McCloy's was an unfortunate, tone-deaf one. An acknowledgement that innocent people had suffered a great injustice during a perilous wartime situation would no doubt have appeased some critics. In fact, McCloy has a decent, high-minded side as well as his darker characteristics.

In 1945, McCloy felt the people of Hiroshima and Nagasaki should be warned about the imminent atomic bombing, but he failed to get the message through within the Department of War. In contrast, he successfully saved the residents of Rothenburg ob der Tauber, a historic town in southern Germany. In the final days of the war, the Americans had massed large artillery around the city, planning to shell it into submission. When McCloy found out, he immediately intervened with the US general in command, Jacob Devers, and suggested he offer the Germans the chance to surrender. This was accepted and Rothenburg escaped destruction. McCloy did not know the medieval town, but later said his mother had visited it, and was a great admirer of the place.

After the war, McCloy worked tirelessly for many years to build a free and democratic Federal Republic and to foster thriving transatlantic relations. At the time, this was by no means everyone's position.

There were many who leapt to McCloy's defense when the controversy erupted. His strongest defenders were Goldman himself, along with Graham Allison, dean of the Kennedy School of Government, home to the McCloy Fellowship. In op-eds and long briefing papers the two men argued passionately that the McCloy name should be retained.

In a letter to the then Harvard president, Goldman made the case for the defense: on the internment of Japanese Americans, Goldman wrote, one has to take into account the prevalent "wartime mentality" after Pearl Harbor. Moreover, McCloy only carried out a decision that ultimately was not his own.

It was true, wrote Goldman, that as high commissioner, McCloy authorized an early release for Alfried Krupp, but this was not done arbitrarily. McCloy was adhering to a recommendation from the advisory board on the pardon of war criminals. This body had issued an opinion which, among other things, judged that Alfried Krupp's long sentence had partly resulted from the fact that his father, a far more guilty figure, was by then already seriously ill.

The accusation that McCloy stopped the bombing of Auschwitz is simply wrong. Goldman's father, Nahum Goldmann, the president of the World Jewish Congress, met with McCloy at the Department of War at the time, urgently requesting that the camps be targeted. McCloy, as assistant secretary of state, told him that British permission would be needed, since the planes were based on British soil. London, McCloy told Goldmann, was strictly against any bombing, because the aircraft would need to refuel on the return leg from Poland. The British feared heavy losses in a strike on what was seen as a "non-military target." The formulation may sound cynical in retrospect, given that this was a site where upward of 1.1 million people were murdered.

John J. McCloy (*seated center left* with Guido standing at *center rear*) with the first group of McCloy Scholars in 1983.

To back up his stance, Guido Goldman presented documents and reports from contemporary witnesses. "My father," he wrote, "has always exonerated McCloy from personal responsibility."

Testimony from key witnesses like Nahum Goldmann and Eric Warburg made a substantial difference in the McCloy controversy. Gerhart Riegner was another who weighed in. Riegner was the Geneva representative of the World Jewish Congress, the first person to raise the alarm about the extermination camps, via the famous "Riegner Telegram."

In May 1983, Eric Warburg wrote to the *Washington Post* "as a Jew born and raised in Germany," and a reconnaissance officer for the British and American air forces for four years. A desire to bomb the extermination camps in Poland, Warburg wrote, was all too understandable, but not technically feasible at the time. The bombs would have been dropped from a great height "with small chance of hitting individual buildings where the Holocaust took place."

Nahum Goldmann was quoted repeatedly. In June 1982, two months before his death, he sent enthusiastic congratulations to McCloy on the decision to set up the fund. "Your role in this unique chapter in the postwar history of the relationship between Germany and the Jewish people was always helpful and enlightened," he wrote. "In this regard I would like to pay tribute to you, not only as a friend but also in recognition of all that you did to facilitate my negotiations with Chancellor Adenauer that led to the historic restitution and reparations agreements also some thirty years ago . . . As I have written in my memoirs, you are 'a statesman who has shown great sympathy for Jewish problems.'"

In the summer of 1983, Guido Goldman received representatives of Harvard's Jewish and Asian student associations to discuss the McCloy issue. After friendly discussions, the controversy subsided, and the McCloy name was retained. The John McCloy Fellowship program continues to be a great success, headed by Jim Cooney for almost a quarter of a century.

"MR. PRESIDENT, PLEASE BE PATIENT UNTIL LUNCH"

June 10, 1987 was an important date for Goldman, and not only because it was the date of Harvard's graduation ceremony that year. That June also marked the fortieth anniversary of the announcement of the Marshall Plan, the German Marshall Fund celebrated its fifteenth birthday, and the McCloy Fellowship was entering its fifth year. Moreover, this was the month when the Busch-Reisinger Museum cleared the Adolphus Busch Hall. Unsuitable air conditioning meant its collection of artworks were at serious risk of damage. After the building's renovation, the Center for European Studies would move into Adolphus Busch Hall, its new home.

What could be more appropriate than inviting a prominent German to give the keynote at the graduation ceremony? The last German to do so had been Helmut Schmidt, eight years previously.

Goldman's Harvard colleague Richard Hunt, historian and honorary president of the American Council on Germany, had the idea of inviting President Richard von Weizsäcker to give the speech, and to award him an honorary doctorate on the same day. The proposal was approved by the university and Goldman was enthusiastic. On January 16, 1987, he wrote to Hunt: "Dear Rick: I think it is a wonderful choice and I hope that he accepts." Goldman offered to speak to von Weizsäcker, whom he knew well, about the content of the speech. It would be desirable, said Goldman, if the president might also take the opportunity to say something about the Marshall Plan, "especially since it will be its fortieth anniversary this June."

Goldman was overflowing with ideas for the Weizsäcker visit, which he saw as an opportunity for a great celebration of German-American and transatlantic relations. But he is well aware that von Weizsäcker's appearance could bring problems, since the Nazi era and its aftermath cast a shadow on his name. Alan Dershowitz could have his knives out when he learned of the president's visit. Ever since the McCloy controversy Goldman had been on his guard.

During the Nazi regime, Ernst von Weizsäcker, the president's father, was a state secretary in the German Foreign Office and an SS "Brigadeführer," a senior rank equivalent to brigadier general. He had been arrested in 1947 and put on trial at Nuremberg. Two years later, the war crimes tribunal sentenced him to seven years imprisonment for crimes against humanity, guilty of active participation in the deportation of French Jews to Auschwitz. On review, the sentence was reduced to five. Among his defense lawyers was his son Richard, then a law student. Throughout his life, he described the judgment against his father as "historically and morally unjust."

In 1950 Ernst von Weizsäcker was given early release, on the orders of the legal office of John McCloy, the US high commissioner. On McCloy's team, legal affairs were the remit of Robert Bowie, later the head of Harvard's Center for International Affairs, where Henry Kissinger was his deputy.

Richard von Weizsäcker accepted the invitation to speak at the 1987 graduation. That spring, he invited Goldman for a meeting at the Villa Hammerschmidt, at the time the Bonn office of Germany's president. Their discussion was accompanied by champagne and caviar. While there, Goldman asked a senior official whether there was a defense briefing on von Weizsäcker's role in the trial against his father, planning to use it if the issue became controversial at Harvard.

He was told there was no such document, but he did not quite believe it. After all, von Weizsäcker had officially visited Israel in October 1985: it seems implausible that a German president with the name von Weizsäcker would travel to encounter Holocaust survivors without meticulously preparing for critical questions at Nuremberg. But Goldman was told it did not exist and flew home empty handed.

Amazingly enough, for many months there was silence at Harvard regarding the upcoming presidential visit. Then, a few days before June 10, the day when the speech was to be given, an article suddenly appeared in the *Boston Globe*. A relatively unknown history professor alleged that Harvard had failed to learn from past mistakes. This would not be the first time the university had made distressing choices, the article said. Harvard honors had been awarded to dubious recipients in the past. But, it went on, Richard von Weizsäcker marked a new low: an invitation and an honorary doctorate for the defender of a war criminal.

Goldman was alarmed, suspecting the hand of Alan Dershowitz behind the piece. He feared the article might be just the beginning of a more concerted campaign. He immediately called his friend Edgar Bronfman, president of the World Jewish Congress, asking him for an affidavit of support for the president. After all, the WJC had itself already honored von Weizsäcker, pinning the Nahum Goldmann Order of Merit to his lapel. Goldman also contacted Henry Rosovsky, dean of the Faculty of Arts and Sciences, asking whether he should go to the media and publish a counter-article.

Rosovsky advised restraint, fearing any response could cause the dispute to explode, putting it all over the front pages and the television news. Goldman did not think von Weizsäcker would approve of Harvard's strategy of avoidance, but Rosovsky was adamant: best to stay calm and wait for the lunch in honor of the Marshall Plan's fortieth anniversary. This was the occasion von Weizsäcker had been invited for, to take place on the day before his address to the graduating class.

The president arrived in Cambridge on June 9, accompanied by his friend Shepard Stone. The two were coming having spent a few days at Stone's country house in Vermont. The lunch was due to take place in the Busch-Reisinger Museum, not long before the building would be closed and renovated ahead of the CES's arrival. As always, before sitting down to lunch, the guests were invited for a drink in the beautiful inner courtyard, Goldman's staff had prepared things perfectly.

Von Weizsäcker had read the *Boston Globe* article, as Shepard Stone had already discreetly informed Goldman, and was outraged that Harvard did

Guido Goldman, Henry Kissinger, Chancellor Merkel, and Karen Donfried (president of the GMF) at the seventieth anniversary of the Marshall Plan, celebrated in Berlin on June 20, 2017.

Guido Goldmann and Karen Donfried at Guido's seventieth birthday in Washington, DC in 2007.

not defend him with all guns blazing. On seeing Goldman in the museum courtyard, he walked up to him stone-faced, complaining bitterly. Goldman explained that they kept the argument out of the headlines and did not want to play it up. To von Weizsäcker, he said: "Mr. President, there will be an answer, please be patient until lunch."

Then came the moment for Henry Rosovsky to speak. Rosovsky is a Russian Jew, born in Gdansk in present-day Poland, who lost many family members in the Holocaust. In a brief address, Rosovsky said he wanted to read from a speech given by the von Weizsäcker on May 8, 1985, the fortieth anniversary of the capitulation of the German Reich. May 8, 1945, the president had told the German parliament, was a "day of liberation from the inhuman system of National Socialist tyranny." The sentence had made history, and the vast majority of Germans, and above all non-Germans, heard it with enormous relief and joyful approval.

That speech, said Rovosky turning to Richard von Weizsäcker, was "the finest speech delivered anywhere in the postwar world." Rovosky went on to read out passages from the speech, paragraph after paragraph, pointing out the moments where he literally "felt a stone roll off my heart."

Goldman recalled that von Weizsäcker, who could often seem an emotionless man, had tears in his eyes. After lunch, the president apologized to Goldman for his brusque words in the courtyard, saying with satisfaction: "Harvard really knows how to handle these things."

CHAPTER 10

The Art Collector

There are probably very few people who combine utterly different worlds in their own person. But Guido Goldman did just that, skipping along a wandering path through worlds very unalike, worlds usually with few if any points of contact. The Kissingers and Kaisers, and their respective worlds, but also the wealthy circles around the de Ménils and de Gunzburgs, the dancers at the Alvin Ailey American Dance Theater, not to mention the networkers, transatlanticists, civil rights activists, professors, artists, bankers, and social workers, groups which so often live in their own separate spheres. Their own bubbles, even.

In March 2018, Goldman brought these worlds—*his* various worlds—together for three entire days. At Goldman's invitation, one hundred and twenty-five friends and companions, representing numerous facets of his extraordinarily varied existence, came together in Washington, DC. Guests from all walks of life attended the gala celebration at the Interconti Hotel, down on the Potomac waterfront. You could overhear conversations about the opera, others speaking of their latest acquisitions on the art market, others about a classroom project for disadvantaged children, others about Trump's threat to the liberal postwar order.

The extraordinary Judith "Judi" Jamison, former artistic director of the Alvin Ailey American Dance Theater and still an international star, moved grandly through the ballroom amidst her entourage. Seated in the center of the room was Henry Kissinger, now almost ninety-five years old. He and Jamison were the two keynote speakers that evening. Kissinger's was, as Thomas Kleine-Brockhoff, vice president of the German Marshall Fund, remembers it, a very atypical address. On such occasions, Kissinger usually speaks about the general world situation, the big global picture. That night's speech, however, was more personal, expressing Kissinger's deeply felt sympathy for his host in every line, and culminating by saying that Guido Goldman had never asked him for anything. Kissinger always returns to that sentence whenever he is asked about Goldman. For a world figure like Kissinger, a former occupant of high office,

The greatest *ikat* coat from the collection.

Guido with Judi Jamison at the Ikat Celebration in Washington, DC (March 2018).

there must be few people who approach you for entirely unselfish reasons. For Kissinger, Goldman's selflessness was evidently a special sign of friendship.

Goldman had deliberately arranged this disparate get-together in order to momentarily blend all these worlds with yet another one, a world which was close to his heart and which loomed large in his life: the world of *ikats*. A world largely unknown to his other friends, but very dear to him.

The occasion for the celebration was the exhibition of works from Goldman's extensive collection of nineteenth century Uzbek *ikats*, held at both George Washington University's new Textile Museum and the Arthur M. Sackler gallery, at the Smithsonian. As well as an exhibition tour, guests could make the short drive to Virginia to visit the collection's warehouse, which uses advanced technology to preserve the sensitive art textiles.

Ikat is a Malay term meaning to wrap or tie, more specifically referring to a weaving technique found in central, east, and southeast Asia, used mainly for clothing, scarves, and tapestries. The origins of the practice go back to sixth- and seventh-century Japan, in the Asuka period. The basic skills involved can also be found elsewhere in the world.

Different methods are used, the most complex of which ties off individual threads or entire bundles into sections, before painting them or dipping them into dye. A variety of colors can thus be combined all along the thread or tied bundle, with uncolored portions also used in the pattern. When the threads are interwoven, extremely complex designs can be created, using a mixture of regular and irregular motifs.

This mode of weaving developed and spread over millennia. By the nineteenth and twentieth centuries, its focus was in Central Asia, in the market towns and cultural metropolises of the old Silk Road, especially Samarkand and Bukhara. This was originally a folk art which crossed and intertwined religious lines. In Bukhara, Jews were mostly responsible for dyeing, because they were permitted to get their hands dirty, while Muslims specialized in weaving. Beginning with the creation of the Soviet Union in the late 1910s, *ikat* art came to a standstill for several decades. Most Jewish dyers left Bukhara, often headed for Palestine. Their accumulated knowledge, skills, and technology were not passed on.

Goldman grew up surrounded with European art. Walking from his childhood bedroom to his parents' living room, he passed impressionist and post-impressionist masterpieces, canvases by Monet and Renoir and Chagall. As a child, he collected art postcards. Bored on Sunday excursions to the Metropolitan Museum and the Museum of Modern Art, dragged around by his parents, he would look forward to adding to his collection of small images.

The postcards, unlike his parents' paintings or works in museums, gave him a very personal relationship with the visual arts. It was in these small postcards that he truly discovered composition, formal interplay, and the psychological impact of color. Above all, the power and magnificence of color fascinated Goldman, and he began collecting at an early age. At first this was in quite an eclectic mode: he bought paintings by Bernhard Schultze and rare posters from Europe, steel sculptures by David Smith and Anthony Caro, and ceramics from Clarice Cliff. But it was Uzbek *ikats* which would, more than anything, put a magical spell on the young Guido Goldman, an enchantment to last for decades more.

His particular love for *ikats* came down—like so much in Goldman's aleatory life—to mere chance. At some point in 1973, Goldman was going down Madison Avenue in a taxi, staring pensively out at the great wall of grey buildings. Then, as if from nowhere, the monotony was broken by a gallery window, containing something large and bright, with shining colors. Goldman was both visually dazzled and emotionally touched.

He stopped the cab and walked over for a closer look. The color and composition reminded him of paintings by Wassily Kandinsky; Goldman was a lover of the Russian's early work, heavily influenced by folk art. But this was not Kandinsky, and it was not painting. It was, he saw, a very large work made of textiles.

Goldman walked up the steps of the Martin & Ullman gallery, looking to discover what it was. The owner, Gail Martin, explained that it was a nineteenth-century *ikat* from Uzbekistan, a country Goldman had then never heard of. Decades later, he remembered with amazement: "I probably couldn't have found Uzbekistan on a map back then."

He was immediately fascinated by the colors and forms of the textile works. As for Kandinsky, many decades later, Goldman was still convinced of at least a visual connection between the strong color and form of the Uzbek fabrics and the Russian's colorful landscapes and figurative images. There is no hard evidence that Kandinsky learned from the Uzbek production, although he probably owned a couple of hand-woven *ikat* coats.

Goldman bought the fabric on the spot, paying a few hundred dollars, then hung it on the wall near the library of his Cambridge apartment. Thus began his *ikat* collection. Twenty-five years later, he owned the world's largest collection, around four-hundred pieces. The encounter also marked the beginning of a long friendship with Gail Martin, who became his *ikat* advisor and curator, guiding him through the works worth buying and those better left alone.

Drawn in particular to the interplay of colors, Goldman acquired his first *ikats* on hunches and feelings. Decades ago, *ikats* were largely unknown and not particularly expensive. Prices rose only when Goldman started buying more and more of them, and others also began to enter the market. By now, there are few remaining *ikats* on the market, and most of those available are in less than perfect condition.

Over time, Goldman became an expert on *ikats*, as well as an *ikat* fan. As with everything in his life, every new interest, he approached the subject in an intense manner, researching *ikat* sales and driving long distances to meet with dealers. Happily, one particularly experienced *ikat* dealer was based in

Central Asian *ikat* from the Goldman collection.

Karlsruhe, in southwest Germany, where Goldman was a frequent visitor to Alex Möller, who lived in the city. Möller, of course, was the former German finance minister with whom Goldman negotiated the establishment of the German Marshall Fund, and who had been a friend ever since.

It was very important to Goldman that the dealers offer him only entire, undivided *ikats*. Frequently, sold pieces were taken from larger wholes—over the centuries, many *ikat* coats and tapestries have been cut into small scarves. In addition, Goldman collected only *ikats* woven before 1870, when colors were made naturally, without any chemical additives.

These older *ikats* are particularly sensitive textiles; protection from bright light, moisture, and excessive heat is essential. In addition, the *ikats* must be properly rolled for storage, without kinks or other irregularities, which might lead the fabric to tear. For his collection, Goldman converted two rooms in the basement of his Concord residence into preservation-standard *ikat* storage, under the expert guidance of the Boston Museum of Fine Arts textile department.

Goldman was increasingly frustrated that his ever-growing collection was not available to be seen by others. In the mid-1990s, he bought a 400-square-meter loft in Manhattan: the central space was large enough to exhibit around a dozen tapestries. Goldman's architect completely redesigned the loft space, under the supervisory eye of gallery owner Gail Martin. Everything in the space was geared toward the *ikats*: acid-free paint on the walls, sophisticated air conditioning, and alarm technology, window blinds with automatic light regulation and dust reduction, even specially developed textile-hanging technology. Smoking was prohibited, and guests were even forbidden to make sudden movements, for fear they might create a draught, move the *ikats*, and damage the fragile textiles.

All this work and expensive investment aimed at a single goal, perhaps even a struggle: Goldman wanted the status of *ikats* as art to be recognized within the art world, no longer dismissed as mere handicraft. In his view, these textiles were as expressive as paintings by Kandinsky or Matisse, and could not be reduced to merely a sophisticated application of technology.

In nineteenth-century Uzbekistan, a weaver did not sit at a loom and randomly begin to weave. The *ikat* masters had minds as artistic and creative as they were mathematical, holding formal designs and chromatic interplay in their heads. For Goldman, these works are akin to paintings carried out with textiles, comparable in the impact of color and in the strongly individual expression. This aesthetic individuality is reflected in the fact that every *ikat* is different: not all are technically perfect and none are completely alike.

Whenever a museum sought to exhibit his Uzbek collection, Goldman insisted that the works be displayed in the picture gallery and not the textiles department. "Fabrics, no matter how skillfully and artistically made," Goldman said of the medium, "are often neglected by museums, and only hung in the farthest corner."

Some thought him a fantasist and strongly disagreed with his enthusiastic assessment of *ikats* as artworks. Even in the late 1990s, the respected textile art magazine HALI dismissed *ikats* as "relatively commonplace types of antique oriental weavings."

Goldman remained stubborn in his commitment, putting together a first-class team to document his collection and assess its value. Well-known art photographer Don Tuttle built a large scaffolding in order to photograph every work in its full beauty. Kate Fitz Gibbon and Andy Hale, experts in Central Asian weaving, traveled to Uzbekistan, Russia, and elsewhere, at Goldman's expense, collecting historical material about *ikats*, research ultimately published in *IKAT: Splendid Silks of Central Asia—The Guido Goldman Collection*. The book was awarded the George Wittenborn Memorial Prize for best art book of 1997, by the Organization of Art Librarians of North America.

This marked a decisive breakthrough for Goldman's collection, and for the acceptance of *ikats* as art. Some of the works in the book went on tour, with exhibition stops at the Boston Museum of Fine Arts, the de Young Museum in San Francisco, the Arthur M. Sackler Gallery in Washington, DC, the Jewish Museum in New York, the Art Institute of Chicago, and the Denver Art Museum.

At every opening, the Uzbek ambassador proudly gave a short address. This approval was extremely important, given heated contemporary debates on looted art in the art and museum world. There is often good reason to ask critically if some of the treasures scattered in museums and collections around the world should not be sent back to their homeland, given their provenance in looting raids. Colonialism in general often ran roughshod over national sensitivities and questions of cultural heritage. Sometimes, it was simply the rich coming in and taking advantage of the poverty of the artists that produced the works.

Striped Central Asian *ikat* from the Goldman collection and cover of the prize-winning catalogue.

Guido Goldman with Uzbek Ambassador Sodyk Sofaev at a US museum exhibition in 1998 in which Goldman was elected to the Uzbek Academy of the Arts.

However, Uzbek art historians and the government were happy with Goldman's *ikat* collection and gave their support to the exhibitions. All too often they had seen *ikats* fall into the wrong hands, ending up sewn into decorative cushions and tablecloths. Goldman, who never visited Uzbekistan, was made a member of the Uzbek Academy of Arts, the first foreigner to receive that honor.

As they became more visible, *ikats* consistently grew in popularity. Their colorful designs were copied, industrialized, and mass-produced, and often ruined in the process. Much more optimistically, and not least thanks to Goldman, Uzbekistan is now returning to its own weaving tradition, with old skills coming back into use. Thousands of new jobs have been created, especially in the Fergana Valley. One particularly famous *ikat* buyer has been fashion czar Óscar de la Renta, who saw examples hanging in Goldman's New York loft and immediately drew inspiration from the patterns and colors.

Guido Goldman and Henry Kissinger at the Ikat Celebration in March 2018, at which Kissinger was the guest speaker, together with Judi Jamison.

In 2015 Goldman sold his Manhattan apartment, gradually donating his now famous *ikat* collection to a handful of art museums. Most have gone to the Sackler Gallery, part of the National Museum of Asian Art. But a substantial number went to the new Textile Museum of the George Washington University in Washington, DC. The latter donation was, in a way, astonishing: Goldman had always rebuffed textile museums, feeling they could not do justice to the *ikats*. Nonetheless the old GW museum received twenty pieces; there was no space to exhibit more in their building.

But that changed suddenly with the construction of the university's new textile museum. (The old one was bought by Amazon founder Jeff Bezos, who converted it into a private residence.) Visiting the opening of the museum as an invited guest, Goldman was excited, almost overwhelmed. The new building, with its modern, understated architecture, high, bright spaces and clear forms,

Bruce Baganz presenting Guido with the Hewitt Myers Award.

seemed to have nothing in common with gloomy, claustrophobic textile museums of the past.

Goldman believed that this new temple of textile art was a worthy home for his *ikats*. This new museum had come into existence largely thanks to one person: Bruce Baganz, a Texas entrepreneur, art collector, and chairman of the board of trustees of the new museum. He shared Goldman's passion for *ikats*, and had the necessary determination and organizational gusto to rebuild the museum, doing everything to make sure the textiles could really shine.

Goldman was so impressed by Baganz's commitment that he made a personal donation of his sixty-eight most beautiful *ikats* to the museum. Of course the man from Houston was at the forefront when Goldman's eclectic worlds met up in Washington, DC in March 2018 for the celebration of the *ikat* as an artform. In the *Washington Post*, the award-winning art critic Sebastian Smee wrote of the Goldman Collection of Uzbek scarves: "They're everything Henri Matisse was trying to achieve, just in colored thread."

CHAPTER 11

The Alvin Ailey American Dance Theater

NO, THEY WANT THE ELVIS IMPERSONATOR

The opening of the new American embassy at the Brandenburg Gate in Berlin made a big splash, literally, although perhaps not the kind its organizers wanted. On July 4, 2008—American Independence Day—rain fell nonstop from the Berlin sky. The two keynote speakers, Chancellor Angela Merkel and former US president George H. W. Bush, father of then president George W. Bush, huddled together under a large black umbrella. By the time they spoke, quite a few guests had wandered off in search of dry land.

Even though the weather was bad on the day, the transatlantic mood was turning brighter. The US embassy was finally back where it was before the war, and German-American relations, badly strained not long before by the Iraq war, were beginning to improve. George W. Bush—an unpopular figure with Germans and Americans, who had launched a devastating war based on lies—would soon be gone from the White House. Barack Obama, a Democrat and an opponent of the war, seemed likely to succeed him.

Obama also had an appearance in Berlin in July, speaking to Germans and to Europeans from in front of Berlin's famous Victory Column, his gaze turned to the Brandenburg Gate. The prospect of the first Black US president was an inspiration to millions, including Guido Goldman.

Since 1994, Goldman had sat on the board of trustees of the Alvin Ailey American Dance Theater, a world-famous New York dance company. The majority of the ensemble's performers are Black, most of them African American. The dancers had often told Goldman about the difficulties and discrimination they faced, four decades after civil rights legislation had brought legal equality. He also came to understand the symbolic force the election of a Black man as US head of state would have for them.

Goldman traveled to the embassy opening ceremony in 2008. The following day, however, was a far more important one for him, when Berlin organized a large festival in celebration of America, under the slogan "Welcome home." As part of the festival, Ailey II—the troupe featuring young talents at the Alvin Ailey American Dance Theater—performed on a stage by the Brandenburg Gate. Goldman had desperately wanted the young dancers to perform at this festival, so important for German-American relations. He did everything in his power to ensure it happened, including paying for most of the dancers' travel expenses.

The following day, July 5, the weather gods changed their tune, and tens of thousands of Berliners flocked happily to the Brandenburg Gate in brilliant sunshine. To the sound of rock, blues, and gospel, the Ailey II dancers moved across the stage—scurrying, running, jumping, striding, fluttering, floating. They bent, stretched, and bent again, tangling and rolling across the surface of the ground, crouching in a circle as if warming themselves by a fire, then flying apart in all directions, like sprays of water from a fountain. Thematically, the usual pieces the company performs encompass slavery and liberation, suffering and happiness, pain and redemption, longing and hope, faith and love.

Alvin Ailey, himself African American, founded the dance theater in 1958 because Black dancers could not find places within the American cultural scene. From the very start, his works came with a clear message, not propounded obsessively, sometimes approached casually or obliquely, but always there, and always presented with a purpose. "When you go on stage, are you making a political statement?" Alvin Ailey was often asked. His answer was clear: "Of course! I'm a Black man. As soon as I stand there, you have an opinion of me."

Born in Texas in 1931 to a seventeen-year-old mother and raised in great poverty, Alvin Ailey experienced hatred and discrimination twice over: as a Black man, but also as a gay man. He died of AIDS in 1989, at the age of fifty-eight.

The final piece the Ailey II troupe performed on that day in Berlin was entitled "Revelations." The piece, first staged by Ailey in 1960, merges personal experience, political messages, choreographic ingenuity and dance skills, creating a great work of art. "Revelations" is a reflection of the dance company's spirit, its essence, its extraordinary emotionality. These characteristics are the calling card of any Alvin Ailey American Dance Theater production, whether performed by up-and-coming young dancers or the main troupe. "Revelations" forms the grand finale of almost every performance, its last resounding chord.

On that day, thousands of Berliners leapt to applaud the ensemble for many minutes. Goldman was overjoyed and went to join the dancers' celebrations and later have dinner with Sylvia Waters, Ailey II's artistic director and his good friend of many years. But there was something Goldman was unaware of: among many people celebrating Ailey II was Jeff Rathke, a young American diplomat. Ten years later, given the thumbs up from Guido Goldman, he would be elected president of the American Institute for Contemporary German Studies.

At the time of the Brandenburg Gate performance, Goldman was not acquainted with Rathke. But Rathke knew a lot about Goldman: for months his embassy colleague Helena Finn, closely involved in the preparations, had been telling him nonstop how great the Alvin Ailey company were.

Here again, apparently separate threads of Goldman's life knitted together perfectly: Finn had met Goldman not long before, a chance meeting at a 2007 dinner hosted by Avrom Udovitch, Goldman's childhood friend, now a professor of medieval Arabic trade history at Princeton. At some point in the evening, Goldman arrived, and proceeded to speak passionately about the Alvin Ailey American Dance Theater and its upcoming tour of Germany. She took great interest, says Finn, because she would be moving to Berlin in a few weeks, where she had been posted to the US embassy.

Not long after, in November 2007, on another visit to Berlin, Goldman invited friends and acquaintances to a dinner to celebrate his seventieth birthday. To Helena Finn's surprise, she found herself on the guest list. During dinner, the idea was mooted of having the Alvin Ailey American Dance Theater perform at the July 4 ceremony. But the theater's main troupe was fully booked, so Goldman proposed bringing Ailey II to Berlin instead. Finn had a word with the right people at the German Foreign Ministry and the Berlin Senate; everyone thought it was a wonderful idea. Only the US ambassador to Germany remained unconvinced. William Timken, an Ohio businessman, Finn recalls, was very keen to book an Elvis Presley impersonator for July 4.

Finn, Goldman, and everyone involved in the preparations were bitterly disappointed at the ambassador's preference, but decided to book Ailey II for the following day, so they could perform as part of the celebration with the people of Berlin. Just as well: had they performed on July 4, it would have been, almost literally, a wash-out.

A SPRUNG FLOOR FOR THE DANCERS

As with painting and sculpture, Goldman's life has been suffused with music, beginning in early childhood. His father loved Beethoven, Mozart, and Bach, his parents often took their sons to operas or concerts in New York, and they were frequent visitors to the Salzburg Festival in summer. The young Guido Goldman tried his hand at the piano, but what came out was a half-hearted mess; he did not really have the talent for it. Picking out the notes was not his thing, and neither was classical music that much. Goldman went to the theater, but not very often. As an adult, he became interested in blues and jazz and built up an extensive record and CD collection. But only the visual arts ever really captured his heart.

When you asked Goldman whether he regretted anything important in his life, if there was anything he would do differently if he had it all again, he would say without hesitation: "I wouldn't wait until 1994 to go and watch dance theater, I wish I had discovered it thirty-six years previously."

Thirty-six years earlier would be 1958. In that year, Goldman was in his junior year at Harvard. His brother Michael, a friend of one of the dancers, actually invited him to the first performance of the newly founded Alvin Ailey Dance Theater (the word "American" was added later), scheduled for the Young Men's Hebrew Association, a meeting point for young Jews in New York. Michael's friend was his future wife Jacqui Walcott, later Jacqui Walcott-Goldman, already a star dancer at a young age. Alvin Ailey had managed to entice her away from the legendary Katherine Dunham Dance Company, led by the eponymous Dunham, a pioneer of Black dance.

However, Goldman turned down the invitation, imagining the performance would be like classical ballet, a parade of flats and tutus. He had no conception of modern dance at that point, nor did he inquire, thus missing an opportunity he would come to regret so much.

The main difference between ballet and modern dance, in a nutshell, is that ballet tries to overturn the laws of gravity, while modern dance seeks to make use of them in very specific ways. Ballet dancers, their bodies extended, strive upward, appearing to float like silk in the wind. Whereas the actions of bending and sinking are more central to modern dance, movements that are always heading groundward. You could say modern dance is literally more grounded. Ballet is also far more regulated by convention, while movement in modern dance is freer and more improvised.

"Grounding" was Alvin Ailey's leitmotif concept. Dancers should not look to take off into the sky, he felt: their message and movements must be understandable to everyone. "For Ailey, modern dance was always about accessibility," says Judi Jamison, the ensemble's great star for many decades, who became artistic director at the request of the terminally ill Ailey in 1989. "You don't dance in a vacuum, you dance for people," Ailey told everyone, over and over again.

Born in 1943, Jamison is now seventy-seven years old, still a bundle of strength, teeming with ideas. Goldman's long-time close associate has a powerful voice which fills a room, her loud, engaging laughter makes glasses clink. But if she does not like a phrase or a question, she will tell you, and put you brusquely back on the right track. "A Black dance theater? Did you just say we are a Black dance theater?" she says indignantly to me at one point: "Mister, Asians and Europeans also dance here, we are a dance theater for everyone." Her strict reactions, tempered by her big heart, have led her ensemble to call her the "gentle tiger."

Alvin Ailey revolutionized modern Black dance. Although he intended his dance theater to primarily use Black performers, he did not share the exclusivity which underpinned the Katherine Dunham Dance Company. In a foreword to the photo book "Ailey Spirit," Wynton Marsalis—renowned jazz trumpeter and director of Jazz at Lincoln Center—wrote that Ailey believed deeply "that the Afro-American sensibility was national, not for 'Negroes only.'. . . Recognizing the democratic power of individualism, Ailey respected diversity in the appearance and movement of each dancer."

Goldman met Ailey only once, briefly, in 1985, and never got to know him. But it was the choreographer's human and philosophical worldview, and his active hatred of the cancer of racism, which brought Goldman to dance theater in 1994, five years after Ailey's death. Since he was a child, deliberately taking the Black elevator with his nanny Ruth, Goldman had known something must fundamentally change in society. "If the dance troupe that Alvin Ailey founded had not been a primarily Black one," said Goldman, "I probably wouldn't have got involved." His dismay at blatant injustice, even more than his enthusiasm for dance and music, was what first led him to the Alvin Ailey American Dance Theater.

Whatever the exact mix of motivation, Goldman immediately agreed when his friend Phil Laskawy, head of auditors at Ernst & Young and chair of the dance theater's board of trustees, asked him to come on board. It helped that the invitation arrived when Goldman was moving his base from Harvard to New York, necessary because of the full-time demands of the investment trust First Spring.

For his first year on the board, Goldman said, he was quiet as a mouse at meetings, thinking he had no idea about modern dance. He became more involved when Judi Jamison, as artistic director, complained about increasing injuries among dancers. Goldman asked to know why. "Because we don't dance on sprung floors," said Jamison, referring to the shock-absorbing underlayer common in dance studios. With only hard floors in the company's studios and stages, dancers could easily sprain an ankle or even break a foot when jumping. Good, springy, yielding parquet is the best, explained Jamison. "But what does that cost?" asked Goldman. "We just have no money for it," interrupted Laskawy, the chairman, telling Goldman he could either pay for it himself, or the discussion was over.

At that time, the dance company was as good as bankrupt. It had to pay cash for every single purchase, right down to the smallest make-up supplies, even pizza from the Italian place nearby. Ailey was a brilliant artist, but finances were not really his thing. He particularly loathed fundraising, says Judi Jamison: a salesman he was not. But the dance operations that he loved cost a lot of money, even when there was none immediately at hand, and the company would have to turn to a bank or private philanthropist.

After the board meeting, Goldman asked Jamison the price of a sprung floor, which turned out to be $35,000. "Okay," said Goldman, "I'll buy it." Judi Jamison still remembers how her jaw dropped in amazement.

A trustee's usual job is to pore over the balance sheets, think about possible donors, and keep a close eye on future finances. "But in Guido Goldman," says Jamison, "we got a trustee, for the first time ever, who was concerned about how every dancer was doing."

Goldman would soon go on to purchase a second sprung floor, this one foldable and portable, to additionally protect the dancers' bones while they were on tour. The company traveled a lot, not only within the United States, but all over the world.

The company has given guest performances in South Africa, China, and Israel, in Paris, London, Berlin, and Saint Petersburg. Every so often on these tours, Goldman would show up out of the blue, watch the performance, go out to dinner with the ensemble, pay hotel bills if they are too much for a tight budget, and bring the dancers on city tours. All at his own expense, of course. For the "white nights" of Saint Petersburg—the summer nights when the sun does not set—he invited the entire crew on a boat trip on the Neva.

Guido with Harry Belafonte and Frances Davis (Miles's widow) in Los Angeles in the early 1990s.

After performances, Goldman would also go backstage from time to time, to make sure things are OK with those who worked outside the spotlight, the ones who have to take apart the scenography and clean up after everyone else. Goldman sent a masseur on tour and would occasionally pay off a dancer's debts.

The dance troupe around Jami Jamison and Sylvia Waters grew very dear to Goldman's heart, who loved to soak up the company's unique esprit. He admired their talent, their free way of life, their ease and lack of concern with convention. The dancers were allowed to use his apartments in New York and Miami; at least once a year he held a big party for them in his *ikat* display space in the Manhattan loft. Goldman ultimately became a vice chairman of the board of trustees, later saying these times were some of the best of his life.

The second half of the 1990s was a time of upheaval for the Alvin Ailey American Dance Theater. At one point, Goldman went with the company to the Spoleto Festival in Charleston, South Carolina, which is great performing

Guido with Desmond Richardson and Dwight Rhoden, stars of the Alvin Ailey American Dance Theater and founders of the Complexions Dance Theater.

talent show as much as a festival, a place where people watch each other's work and exchange ideas.

At a meeting held in a church, Goldman heard Jamison give a speech about the dance theater and her dreams for the future, and passionately pleading for help to acquire a permanent home for the troupe. What the Alvin Ailey American Dance Theater needed was a permanent New York location, she said, to practice undisturbed and develop new talent, with enough space to host dance initiatives for the neighborhood and nearby schools. A permanent home, she concluded, was almost essential for the dance company to survive.

Goldman was both surprised and impressed by the idea, caught by the fire of Jamison's imagination. Back in New York, he spoke with Phil Laskawy, and they proposed to the board that Joan Weill set up a small search committee to find suitable donors. But Weill, the spouse of philanthropic Citibank boss Sandy Weill, turned down the offer. But Laskawy did not give up, hitting on the bright idea of offering her his own job to attract her on board. Soon enough,

Guido with the great Alvin Ailey star dancer, Renee Robinson.

Guido with Alvin Ailey star dancers, Judi Jamison and Sarita Allen.

Weill was indeed elected the new chair of the trustees, a position in which she raised enormous sums—around $100 million—in record time.

So it was, in 2005, the Alvin Ailey American Dance Theater moved into its new home on 55th Street and 9th Avenue. The Joan Weill Center for Dance, a seven-story glass tower in the heart of Manhattan, is the largest dance center in America, with over seven thousand square meters of floor space. Goldman donated the fitness room, as well as a large mosaic-portrait of Judi Jamison. The image adorns a wall on the fifth floor, the day-to-day training space for the thirty or so people who make up the theater's core team. Goldman wanted the portrait to preserve Jamison's memory, as the woman who saved the ensemble from ruin after Ailey's death, turning it into one of the world's leading dance theaters.

Jamison retired in 2011, and Goldman himself retired from the board three years later. But Goldman remained tightly connected to the dance theater, which he called his "family of the heart." To the end of his life, well into his eighties, he continued to treasure the dance theater, regarding its unique history and extraordinary performances as something to be cherished and cared for, a kind of national shrine—all the more so in 2020, when it became dramatically clear that racism was very much alive and well in America, not least from a president in the White House who incited hatred with relish.

For Goldman, concern for the health and well-being of the dancers remained central. He did not just worry about the Alvin Ailey company, although he continued to suggest that its fitness room was too small and underequipped. Goldman also funded a dance teacher and a studio for an elementary school in the Dorchester neighborhood of Boston. Here, his friend Meg Campbell—a Harvard teacher he knew through his college friend John Mudd—had started a very unusual school project, the Codman Academy Charter School.

Dorchester was and is home to many very poor families, most of them of color, and including many immigrants from the Caribbean and Africa. Many children there have food access problems and can suffer endemic illnesses, including psychological problems. One very unusual thing about the Dorchester school was its literal connection to the local health center, with which it shared space. In the corridors, and at lunch in the cafeteria, schoolchildren mixed with doctors and nurses.

It was Goldman's idea to set up a dance studio for the school. Meg Campbell was immediately in favor: dancing, she says, helps alleviate worry, allowing children to feel elated and carefree for a short moment. On any given day here, dozens of children delightedly storm around the small dance studio on the first floor of a brick building, across from the health center. Their black shoes, with small metal plates on the soles, front and back, are stored on large wooden shelves. During half-hour lessons, the noise of tap shoes builds up gradually: tack-tack-tack-tack, faster and faster. As airy and fleet-footed as tap can look, it requires a particularly high level of musicality, perseverance, and rhythm. As one Dorchester teacher put it: "The body and soul must be in harmony."

Shortly before his death, Goldman also donated $300,000 to the renowned Batsheva Dance Company in Israel. The dance theater was having a new campus constructed in Tel Aviv, and Goldman was particularly keen to see a modern health center in one of the buildings.

Here is yet another example of Goldman's connections stretching across different worlds: Baroness Bethsabée de Rothschild, whose family, like the Goldmanns, fled the Nazis to New York, was among the founders of contemporary dance theater in Israel. Her father Edouard and brother Guy de Rothschild were friends with Goldman's father Nahum Goldmann. Martha Graham, another modern dance icon, helped to establish the Batsheva Dance Company. One of her students was Alvin Ailey.

In 1990, Ohad Naharin, a friend of Goldman's, was appointed as artistic director of the Israeli ensemble. Naharin's wife Mari Kajiwara was in turn a great star with the Alvin Ailey American Dance Theater: when she died of cancer in late 2001, the *New York Times* dedicated a long obituary to her, especially her work with Alvin Ailey.

These three dance theaters—Graham, Ailey, and Batsheva—have always shared a single ideal. They regard modern dance, contemporary dance, as something more than high art; it also comes with important social functions. Moreover, their founding principles include the idea that dance should be a home for all its performers, regardless of skin color, religion, or sexual orientation.

Goldman emphasized that his philanthropic donation to the Batsheva—a multiethnic and multidenominational dance company—was primarily because of his friend Ohad Naharin and out of concern for the dancers' health. But he did not deny that his donation could send a political message, at least in passing, directed against growing nationalism and increasing intolerance in Israel, in the country that his father did so much to help found and where he was laid to rest on Mount Herzl.

CHAPTER 12

What Remains?

March 2020: by now, Guido Goldman and I have had some two dozen formal conversations. We are coming toward the end of our final interview, and the voice recorder is running one last time. As always, we are sitting in the kitchen, his favorite room in the Concord house.

Many trees are visible through the large, floor-to-ceiling windows, part of the small forest that slopes down to the Concord River behind the terrace. The sculptures in the garden are veiled, winter not yet gone, although spring can be felt, gradually breaking through. A red cardinal lands on a branch in front of the window, puffs up its feathers and flies away.

Goldman loves this house, the view, the tranquility. This place is so peaceful that it is almost possible to forget the emerging disaster outside. The coronavirus pandemic has only begun to claim its hundreds of thousands of American victims, President Trump continues to incite hatred, Joe Biden's victory is nowhere in sight, and the cancer of nationalism is still growing nearly everywhere, including in Europe.

If he were in better health, and not almost eighty-three years old, Goldman says that he and his friend Karl Kaiser would approach the president of Harvard and the dean of Arts and Sciences. As in the late 1960s, when they came up with West European Studies, he would demand that Harvard do more for the study of Europe and Germany. Knowledge about the European continent is dwindling, complains Goldman. Regional studies are no longer being taught, although it remains vital to understand other societies and political systems.

Goldman knows he's tilting against windmills here, setting his face against an unstoppable trend. New generations have new perspectives. Visions and missions change with the times, as do the institutions where they are anchored. "I'm a twentieth-century man," says Goldman, "I was sixty-three when the twenty-first century began. No one can tell me I had my biggest achievements in the last twenty years."

He leans back in his large black desk chair, rocking slightly. He always sits on that chair in the kitchen, always in the same place, at the head of the large table, on the left-hand side. Outside the window, the red cardinal has returned and settles at the edge of the terrace. "Isn't it a bit early in the year for the bird?" Goldman says. The winter has been very mild, like most recent winters.

Climate change spares nowhere, not even peaceful Concord. Goldman points out that water shortages, epidemics, and refugee migrations have a direct impact on foreign, domestic, and defense policy and are a "very big issue" for the institutions he has been involved with.

But Goldman also criticizes how the issue is discussed: the tone is too moralistic, he says, and the demands too absolute. He cannot accept that the sheer size and danger of the problems demand radical solutions only. He wholeheartedly agrees with Fridays for Future, the climate protection movement, he says, and with those calling for a more generous reception for refugees. But societies cannot be stretched beyond breaking point, and other people's views of the world's problems must be borne in mind. No sane person could seriously want more Trumps to come out of the woodwork, or to see the AfD—the "Alternative for Germany," Germany's right-wing populist party—in power. But states and people act according to their own interests, he concludes, and these have to be explored and then balanced out. "Moralistic dogmatism will not get us one inch further."

Goldman is currently reading the book *1941* by the historian Marc Wortman; it has stimulated his thinking, he says, and he wishes many young people would read it too. In fact, the book is a shocking document, but a realistic one: it describes Franklin D. Roosevelt's tough balancing act between global strategy and domestic policy in the months leading up to the US entry into World War II.

The book recounts how Roosevelt, entirely convinced that Hitler's Germany was a danger to the world and must be stopped, helped the British as best he could, sending weapons and deploying the secret services. But American public opinion, still suffering from World War I, remained opposed to full participation in the war against the Nazis, unwilling to put its own forces at risk. Roosevelt also had to fight off powerful isolationist and anti-Semitic forces in the United States, including some overtly sympathetic to the Nazis, not least Charles Lindbergh's America First Committee.

But the public mood changed overnight with the Japanese attack on Pearl Harbor on December 7, 1941. The following day, the United States entered World War II, declaring war on Japan, whose ally, the German Reich, then declared war on America. "We had to be attacked ourselves first, our own interests had to be impacted," says Goldman, "it was not enough that Hitler was about to subjugate Europe and murder millions of Jews."

Was it wrong to act out of self-interest? Goldman says he does not think so, that's how states and people worked, a fact sometimes forgotten. Then he conjures up a horror scenario of a world where Pearl Harbor never happened. Hitler's criminal regime would have defeated Russia, conquered large parts of Europe and gassed even more Jews. The British would have begged for a peace treaty, the Americans would have negotiated with Hitler.

Fortunately, things turned out differently. For people like Goldman, the catastrophe of World War II also offered an opportunity. Afterward, they were able to put their ideals into practice, building institutions to protect and disseminate them, and establishing a completely new international order.

Goldman's cell phone rings. It is Karl Kaiser, who says he'll be right over. He lives in New Hampshire, a two-hour drive away. Whenever Kaiser has work to do at Harvard, which he frequently still does, he stays with his friend Goldman. The remainder of our interview will have to wait for a couple of hours.

But the discussion does not end here, it continues cheerfully when Kaiser arrives. Like Goldman, he's a deeply political animal. "We are," says Kaiser, referring to himself and Goldman, "products of that bloody century and its transcendence. We grew up in this context, that was the world we became involved with." Kaiser lists off the new challenges presented by the twenty-first century: climate change, the ever-increasing flow of refugees, the re-emerging ethnic conflicts, the digital revolution with all its dramatic consequences. "Guido and I experience all this only as old men. We can have our say, but others will decide what the solutions look like, and how institutions will have to be restructured and realigned in the long term."

The next morning, Goldman says that he lay awake thinking about what Kaiser had said. In fact he felt that his own generation had it easier than today's young people. "Sure, the war was ground zero, an apocalypse, but we were able to create something new when the horror was over. Today it's all about saving existing achievements from destruction."

Goldman feels oppressed by the return of dark forces, and sees his life's work threatened, both from within and from the outside. He would never have thought, he says, that America, his own country, would become a risk factor or that Europe would again be ravaged by nationalism and protectionism. He has no immediate answers on how to counteract these threats.

The institutions he cofounded are neither a form of protest nor a political movement. They may be nongovernmental, but they are set up to cooperate with the states of the Western world, in order to make the world a better place. But how on earth can that work, if states are ruled by the likes of Trump or Viktor Orbán?

This dilemma will not be solved easily, even after Trump's defeat, with Joe Biden moving into the White House. Challenges to the liberal world order will not go away overnight; the United States will never return to the same old role. The balance has shifted too much for that, even without Trump. In 2020, the liberal international order—primarily created and led by Americans after World War II—is less liberal, less international, less orderly, and less American. There are good reasons to look to repair and reinforce it—existential reasons, you could even say—although it would change in form, of course. A value-based international order is more important than ever, given external threats from Russia and China and the danger of internal norm erosion. But this belief is not held universally. Civil society organizations like those established by Guido Goldman have an important role to play here. Within the process of reorientation, they can supply ideas, mediators, and innovators.

Goldman's basement in Concord holds stacks of boxes with photos, thousands upon thousands of images of his life. They show him with his parents and his brother Michael, with Stanley Hoffmann, Karl Kaiser, and Henry Kissinger, with Willy Brandt and Alex Möller, with Ronald Reagan and Helmut Schmidt, with Richard von Weizsäcker and Angela Merkel. In the photo archive, Goldman can be seen at countless conventions, parties, and receptions. The images from the past twenty years include a particularly large number with the dancers of the Alvin Ailey American Dance Theater.

Goldman is proud of what he has created. His transatlantic institutions changed American views of Europe and Germany after the war; they created new transatlantic momentum and enabled German scholars to come and study at Harvard. His *ikats* hang in major art museums, and the dance theater he loved has achieved world fame, now settled happily in its own building in the middle of New York.

Of course, Goldman wants his accomplishments recognized, but he says he played only a small role compared to others he has known. Kissinger became

Guido Goldman with Chancellor Merkel at Harvard Commencement (May 30, 2019).

Secretary of State, Zbigniew Brzeziński was National Security Advisor, Stanley Hoffmann a famous professor, author of innumerable books. Others, like the de Gunzburgs, Engelhards, de Ménils, or Annenbergs have lavishly bestowed funds on museums, libraries, and university buildings.

So would he turn back the clock if he could? Does he wish he had made different choices? Goldman is silent for a moment, leafing through the photo albums lying on the kitchen table, gazing out the window where the March sun is disappearing behind the trees. No, he says, maybe I could have been a government minister, ambassador, university president or full professor, but I made other decisions. The following morning, I leave Goldman's house. A quick coffee at the kitchen table, a hasty recap to be sure we forgot nothing in our conversations, the taxi is waiting outside. This was to be the last time we would ever meet. Just nine months later, Guido Goldman died of cancer, at the age of eighty-three.

Few people know who Guido Goldman is, no institutes are named after him, no signs on buildings with his name. But does that really matter? Guido

The view with fall foliage from Guido Goldman's Concord House.

Goldman's remarkable work and his many achievements were not only marked by extraordinary success, but also by their own special, unique quality. That will remain, long after his own life has come to an end.

Index of People